CW00482548

WALSHY

MY AUTOBIOGRAPHY

WALSHY

MY AUTOBIOGRAPHY

Wouldn't It Be Good

Trinity Mirror Sport Media

For Mum and Dad – for everything you've done for me…

Trinity Mirror Sport Media

Walshy: My Autobiography
Wouldn't It Be Good

© Paul Walsh

Written with David Clayton.

Production Editor: Simon Monk.
Cover Design: Lee Ashun, Graeme Helliwell.
Production: Michael McGuinness, Harri Aston.

First Edition
Published in Great Britain in 2015.
Published and produced by: Trinity Mirror Sport Media, PO Box 48,
Old Hall Street, Liverpool L69 3EB.

Managing Director: Steve Hanrahan
Commercial Director: Will Beedles
Executive Editor: Paul Dove
Executive Art Editor: Rick Cooke
Senior Marketing Executive: Claire Brown
Sales and Marketing Manager: Elizabeth Morgan

ISBN: 978-1-910335-14-7

Photographic acknowledgements:
Tony Woolliscroft, PA, Paul Walsh Collection

Printed and bound by CPI Group (UK) Ltd, Croydon, CR0 4YY.

Contents

CONTENTS

Acknowledgements

I'd like to thank a handful of people for being there at important times in my life and career. I'll start with my mum and dad who would always come and watch me play whenever they could. I loved playing well and showing off when they were there and I think they enjoyed watching me just much. I'd also like to thank John O'Connor, my old manager at Londinium and somebody who was a major influence on my fledgling football career.

Also Roy Passey at Charlton for being straight with me and giving me good values that I carried throughout my playing days. Thanks to the late Alan Sealey who used to drool at some of the things I did on the pitch as a youngster and I loved it. Ian Salter at Charlton for helping me in the later stages of my youth career and because he was a good guy. Also Bill and Pat and Berry at Luton.

Thanks also to my wife Beverly and two sons Mason and Jordan and also John Benson, who I first met before I joined Charlton and who has been a sounding board over the years who tried to help me along in my career and genuinely wanted me to do well. There have been others along the way but these are the people who helped me get to where I wanted to be.

Paul Walsh, Hampshire, April 2015

Foreword

I had followed Paul Walsh's career closely and knew what a terrific player he was so when the opportunity to sign him arose, I didn't hesitate. There was still a lot of work to do, of course, because I was manager at Portsmouth who were then in the Championship and Paul was at Tottenham in the Premier League.

But as it happened, he was looking for a fresh start and Portsmouth was the ideal place for him to find his best form again. We met up, hit it off straight away and he agreed to move to Fratton Park.

Paul had tremendous ability and to get a player of his quality to drop down a division was a real coup for Portsmouth and for me because I thought he was one of the best forwards in the country, even though he would have been the first to admit he'd probably lost his way a little at Spurs.

With the talent Paul had, I knew if we could get him playing anywhere near the levels he played at for Liverpool and Luton, we'd have a hell of a player on our hands.

If anyone had thought he was past his best and maybe on his way out, they couldn't have been more wrong. He arrived at Fratton Park and his energy and enthusiasm was infectious.

What struck me was his determination to make the move work and prove that he wasn't coming to Portsmouth for one last pay day – that was obviously going to be a plus for me and the club.

He was unlucky to pick up a virus very early on and it was a number of weeks before we knew what it was that was leaving him devoid of energy and exhausted all the time. I initially told him it was down to old age, but after tests revealed he was suffering from the virus, he was ordered to rest for a fortnight.

He gradually returned to the energy levels he'd had when he first arrived – and when he really got going, he was integral in making our team tick. He brought the best out of Guy Whittingham and along with Alan McLoughlin and Mark Chamberlain, we had one of the best attacks in the division.

It was a testament to his contribution that Guy scored almost 50 goals that season and it was Paul who was voted Player of the Season by the Portsmouth supporters! I understood the reasons, though because he'd had an outstanding season and I couldn't have asked for more from him.

I think Paul is a really top guy and I've kept in touch with him over the years because I enjoy his company. When I look back over his career, I think he was an outstanding player who was maybe around in the wrong era. His style of play and ability would have put a hefty price tag on him today because make no mistake, he was a huge talent.

His desire to win and his character was top-notch and like many footballers over the years, he may have made the wrong choice on occasion but it doesn't take anything away from the fact that Paul Walsh was an outstanding footballer.

Jim Smith, Spain, September 2014

01

Walking Tall

I suppose throughout my life I've always been a battler, driven to prove anyone wrong who doubted my ability and, more often than not, winning the fight. Whether it was proving coaches wrong, team-mates or – at some of the clubs I played for – the supporters, I was never one to take a setback on the chin.

I'd have to show them they were making a mistake through self-belief and sometimes sheer bloody-mindedness because I was never prepared to give up on my dream of becoming a footballer. Those fighting instincts would serve me well for most of my career.

I grew up in a working-class family in London and had a happy childhood. I was born in Plumstead in 1962, not far from our home in Abbey Wood, a small residential area in the south east of the city. I lived in a fairly modest terraced house with my mum June, dad Don and older brother Mark. My old man was a dyed-in-the-wool West Ham United fan who worked as an electrician at the Bank of England and he always made sure we had everything we needed, as did mum, who worked at Tate & Lyle. Whenever Mark or I really needed something, our parents would do whatever they could to get it for us.

My life was family, friends, football and school, all of which I was settled and very content with. Dad had been a season-ticket holder at Upton Park for many years and some of my earliest memories are of him going on about Geoff Hurst, Martin Peters and Bobby Moore and the football academy over at Upton Park. With that in mind, I suppose I should have grown up a claret and blue but I didn't, though I'd always have a soft spot for them.

Had Dad managed to take me to more games, I would no doubt have ended a Hammer, but I think he wanted to be with his mates more on matchdays so he could have a few beers and just be himself for a few hours without his youngest lad getting into mischief.

I would have gone anywhere to watch a match and frequently did when I got the chance, going to Upton Park one week or climbing over the wall at The Valley to watch Charlton Athletic play the next. But it wasn't until my uncle Malcolm offered to take me to Highbury to watch Arsenal that I finally felt like I'd found my club. He took me a few times and each time I went I couldn't wait to get into the ground and be part of it all.

Each time I knew I was going to watch Arsenal play I would count down the days and hours. It was the early Seventies when I started going to games on a fairly regular basis. Charlie

George was at his peak and by that time and much to my dad's dismay, I was now a fully-fledged Gunner. Still, one Christmas he put London rivalry aside and bought me a pair of white boots similar to ones worn by Arsenal's Alan Ball.

They had two thin black stripes down them and nobody else really wore anything like them me at the time, so I treasured them. Dad would still throw the odd West Ham tracksuit or shirt in there every now and then just to try and sway me towards his beloved Irons.

The thing I remember most about those days was the freedom we had as kids. Initially we'd have to go to family and friends after school, but when Mark was old enough and I was about eight, we sort of looked out for ourselves – with approval from mum, of course. You learned to look after yourself, become streetwise and just get on with it – a world away from the sheltered life my kids have had. It wasn't the worst area of London to live in but it had its rough edges and you had to be able to handle yourself. Even though I was small, I'd never back down, no matter how big the other kid was.

The constant play fights with my brother – who was older and bigger at the time – paid off in the end. He was three years my senior and physically stronger. Because of that he always got the better of me whenever we had a little spat, which would wind me up no end. It toughened me up and taught me how to look after myself, even though I hated it at the time.

My first school was Thomas A Becket Catholic Primary and I'd play football at break time in the playground like the majority of kids my age. My head sports teacher was a guy called Mr Vosper, who wasn't exactly my favourite member of staff. He reminded me of the PE teacher in the 1970s film Kes (played by Brian Glover). I remember when I was aged nine, he made us play on a full-sized pitch with full-sized goals.

There was one time he made up the numbers and tried to go through the whole team at full pelt with a sizeable height and weight advantage in his favour. I half expected him to be giving a third-person commentary as he ran towards goal – 'It's the slightly balding Bobby Charlton on the ball…'

Being a Catholic school with nuns and a strict discipline code, you had to behave or face the consequences, but as Vosper passed me once I said under my breath, 'Why don't you just fuck off?' – exactly as the point he turned to look at me.

Despite my bad timing, I discovered that he didn't totally hold it against me. In fact, he became an unlikely ally as he surprisingly stood up for me when I was being overlooked for the area team a year or so later. I'd been doing well from the primary school XI, he knew I was good and couldn't understand why I hadn't progressed beyond my school side.

So he complained to the manager of the local district team who was also a teacher at a rival school and seemed to favour his own pupils. Vosper told him it was a joke that I wasn't in the team. The captain was a lad called Neil Hudson, who was sort of a rival of mine at the time, and I remember sitting around a table while they had a meeting about me. Vosper wouldn't back down and eventually the other guy agreed I should be given a chance so I started being selected for the district side.

Around that time, most of the teams I played for or came up against were run by teachers whose only motive was to win at all costs. They weren't bothered how they did it, just so long as their team won. There was little in the way of development or tactics and by the age of ten I was still one of the smallest kids in my year. Some of the coaches just didn't believe they could win with me in the side – or refused to try.

It didn't seem to matter that I was technically one of the best players in my age group, it was just how it was. It became a regular disappointment when a kid who was physically bigger than me would get the nod instead of me.

I tried not to lose heart and never give in but there were some days when I would end up totally pissed off with everything. If I was either subbed or started on the bench I would end up going home in a foul mood and giving my mum a hard time.

I would go home with the hump and obviously it was her fault that things hadn't gone my way – I was a stroppy, headstrong little fucker at times and I must have driven her mad.

The only other sport I had more than a passing interest in was badminton, which I used to love playing and seemed to have a natural leaning to. I got into it because my brother played regularly. I started going two or three times a week after school at a local club about 400 yards from my house.

I got a great work-out each time I played because you need fast feet, a good touch, balance, sharpness over short distances and stamina to play the game at a decent level.

A good opponent would have you running all over the court and I was starting to get pretty good – so much so that a guy called Len Green who ran the badminton club at Abbeywood Comprehensive asked me if I fancied competing in the Kent junior badminton championships.

The chance to test myself against players I'd never come up against before appealed to me and I did really well, getting to the final where I was up against a kid who was technically better than me. He didn't have a will to win as strong as me though and I just edged the game to take the title. It was one of the most fantastic days of my life and I remember staring at my winner's medal as Len drove me home, pleased as punch.

I met the same lad again the following year's tournament but this time he got his own back, beating me comfortably in one of the early rounds. It was probably because football had started to take over most of my spare time by that point and the demands that came with it were becoming greater all time.

The time I had for badminton was less and less and, though I loved playing, I had to leave it behind as football took over.

If I wasn't at a game, I'd be playing in one. If there was a patch of grass to play on, me and my mates David Gilligan, Doug Colville and Steve Middleton would be on it playing three and in, Wembley or just kicking it against the wall until the sun went down. We would have carried on in the dark had we not been called in for our tea.

I was a natural show-off who wanted to beat everyone else and score. I practised dribbling, close control and shooting – and I knew I was getting better all the time. There was another piece of land underneath a flyover near our house that I would go to when my mates were busy and play on my own. I would go there at some point almost every day and I suppose it is pretty much where I taught myself to play the game.

There was a huge concrete wall plus a couple of concrete pillars which I used as goals and I would be there for hours at a time. I had my dreams of being famous one day as most kids did, but back then, that's all they were. So long as I had a ball at my feet, I was happy.

02

Happy Valley

By the age of 10 I'd reached the stage where I needed to play for a team other than just my school. I was thinking of joining a Sunday League side called Villa Court Rovers and went along to a trial which went pretty well. Afterwards, the coach asked me to join. Before I played for them, a guy called John O'Connor turned up at our house out of the blue and asked my parents if he could speak with me about joining his team, Londinium – I think my name was starting to get mentioned in local circles and he just took a chance.

John was in his mid-forties and had three grown-up sons but his football team was his passion and I would soon discover that what his club lacked in facilities and equipment, he more than made up for in enthusiasm and ingenuity. He could make things happen on the most threadbare budget you could imagine. I already knew Londinium were a decent side so I said I'd come along to training and take it from there.

It gave my spirits a lift because I'd seen a number of lads in my area being picked up for local teams and I believed I was as good if not better than many of them. I couldn't work out why nobody had asked me to play for them yet.

I hated being overlooked – even when I was just having a knockaround with my mates I wanted to be the one that stood out. John was the perfect coach for me and he came along at exactly the right time.

Londinium was a one-age-group club with just one team and I soon felt at home with John's rag-tag outfit. There was something about Londinium that struck a chord with me and in my first season at the club we won the divisional cup, which at that time was bigger than winning the league.

I scored both goals as we beat Teviot Rangers 2-1 in the final with the second proving to be the winner when I was put clean through and dinked it over the keeper. That was my first football medal and it helped enhance my reputation in Sunday League football. Londinium had a semi-regular home ground at Yarnton Way near Thamesmead.

It was a bit of a concrete jungle around that area. There were high-rise flats at one end of the pitch and a council estate at the other, but we didn't care what the surroundings were like.

While our facilities and kit weren't ideal, our team spirit was brilliant. So what if we weren't as well turned out as some of the other teams? We had bags of enthusiasm, energy and a lot of decent players, too. I suppose the club reminded me of myself, in that nothing seemed to come easily. John pulled everything together by working tirelessly to keep the team going. He'd said to us all on one occasion after training, 'I've got us somewhere to train with a dressing room but we'll need to tidy it up a bit.'

Having changing rooms was something of a luxury, as we'd normally either turn up in our kit or get changed at the side of the pitch. So we went along the next day and there were tins of paint and brushes waiting for us with John there in his overalls encouraging us to get stuck in and help.

We all mucked in, had a great laugh getting it sorted and it was typical of John's unorthodox ways of building camaraderie and togetherness – I suppose created through adversity.

In return, he just wanted us to show that we cared and that playing for his team meant something. He had an FA coaching badge and was more than a decent manager, but it was the extra mile he always went that really made the difference.

He picked up players who lived miles away and driving across London and being a chauffeur for some of the lads when they needed a lift was all part of the service. He'd organise camping weekends and matches away in Europe, all on a shoestring.

I don't know how he managed it in all honesty – maybe it was partly from subs or fundraising events but I don't recall us having to fork out much towards the trips.

On one occasion he drove us all the way to Germany in his minibus where we played 1860 Munich – God knows how he did it all because he had a family of his own to look after. But we loved him for it and would have run through brick walls for him.

While we were in Munich he took us all to the beer festival and bought us a huge stein of beer to share, which left us all a bit worse for wear, but it was great fun. We were staying at the

Olympic Stadium and I was sick when we got back but John didn't mind us enjoying ourselves and larking about, so long as it didn't get out of hand. Then when it came to football he wanted us to focus, enjoy playing and to play the game in the right spirit.

We more than held our own against 1860, drawing the game, while travelling abroad with the team had given me a glimpse of what the life of a footballer might be like. John was always trying to organise some trip or other and not long after he took us to Dunkirk to play a match. He'd arranged for us all to stay with local families.

Me and my partner in crime Glen Burville, who was three weeks younger than I was, went to have dinner at the home of a French family – but they didn't speak a word of English. Glen was just verbally insulting them throughout the meal but they didn't have a clue what he was on about and I was just crying with laughter – it was just one of those things you do as a kid.

We were a nightmare when we were together. Glen would go on to play for West Ham but he was always getting into mischief. When he was around, John knew I wouldn't be on my best behaviour because he always had me in stitches.

For our next European adventure, we travelled to Dordrecht in Holland for a tournament. John had arranged for us to stay with some local Dutch families, but this time he made sure Glen and I were split up.

I stayed with the Vlot family in Dordrecht and really enjoyed my time with them – so much so that I travelled back to see them on my own for a week the following summer, travelling over by ferry before being picked up at the other end.

Back home, I left my primary school Thomas A Becket behind

for good in 1973 and, aged 11, went to Woolwich Polytechnic. I was an okay student without being particularly academic and I was always on the fringe of something or other in class.

Though I wasn't the worst pupil, I was a long way from being the best – the problem was I couldn't concentrate, mostly because I wanted to be out playing football and didn't really want to be there at all.

Physics and chemistry passed me by completely and I'd spend a lot of my time staring out of the window during certain lessons or watching the clock until break, lunch or home time.

The only area of schoolwork I really excelled at was sport. I used to take a tennis ball with me each morning and at break time, I'd kick it around the playground. I'd dribble through the crowds of kids in my steel toecap boots, which no doubt enhanced my dribbling ability and close control, though I didn't realise I was doing that at the time.

I played for the school team and was soon playing a couple of years above my age group. I was still playing for the district team as well, where I was standing out on a regular basis. Eventually, I was picked for the county team which was another couple of notches up, but if I was going to make it, I need to get spotted soon.

Then, the break I needed to kick on again came when a local Charlton Athletic scout called Jim Fibbins watched me for Londinium. He approached me after we'd played against Inter Fico, who had Tony Cascarino, Andy Townsend and Stevie Barker playing for them. Cas was training with Gillingham while Andy and Stevie were on Chelsea's books, so they were a really strong side.

I was aware of all of them, having heard their names

mentioned and because our paths crossed occasionally. There was a mutual, if unspoken, respect between us and I felt a degree of vindication that I'd been scouted in a game against the best team in our league.

Andy was quite a big noise back then, maybe more than anyone else of our age group in the South London area. I'd occasionally come up against other lads who would end up going on to make a name for themselves including Ian Dawes, Warren Neill, Terry Gibson and Tony Finnigan plus many others. Jim invited me along to train with Charlton's junior sides, where I'd be training regularly among kids my age and older.

It was the opportunity I'd been hoping for and now I had a chance I wasn't about to let it slip. I was desperate to kick on and I'd be training under the watchful eyes of several experienced coaches including Roy Passey and Keith Peacock. It was an opportunity to impress but it didn't mean I stopped playing for the other sides I was representing at the time.

Charlton just didn't want to miss out on any local talent that may have been on their doorstep and there was a fair turnover of kids coming and going. Another scout, Tommy Coleman, from Arsenal then asked if I wanted to go and train with them, but getting across London in the rush hour even once a week was not a realistic option so I reluctantly said no.

I was then picked for the London County squad, which was a level up again, but that's where the problems that had held me back initially began to resurface. Due to the fact I was still one of the smallest kids in the group, I wasn't playing many matches.

I was skinny, maybe not much more than nine stone, and the coach at London County didn't think I was strong enough to play against opponents who were physically bigger and stronger than I was.

It irritated the hell out of me if I'm honest because they weren't interested in developing me or some of the other lads who were similarly built. They just wanted the team they put out to win any which way they could. I suppose if they were facing a team of six-foot powerhouses, they were never going to select skill and technique over strength and size.

It was a disease in the English game and it is still around today to a certain extent.

It was a recurring issue for me, too. My mum and dad took me to Loughborough for England Schoolboys trials along with another lad called Richard Smith, who was a strapping, six-foot centre half and massive in comparison with a lot of kids our age. Because of his physique, he was getting into teams all over the place.

There were about 100 or so other kids who'd been invited along and we spent a week going through various training sessions and playing in games. We were sorted into teams arranged in order of ability ranging from A down to E – I was in E so there was no real chance I'd get selected. I did begin to wonder if anyone would ever believe in me and give a chance at a higher level.

I was angry and felt utterly pissed off. Ahead of me were the likes of Terry Gibson, Tommy Caton, Irvin Gernon – another monster for his age – Jimmy Bolton, Shaun Brooks and a number of others, so I was nowhere near playing for England.

I had to watch them play at Wembley in front of 80,000 people or so (which would have been right up my street) – all the time knowing I was as good if not better than some of the ones who'd been selected. I was gutted I hadn't been given that chance.

There was still hope, though. I found Roy Passey at Charlton to be the best coach I'd played under yet. He was hard, direct but fair, loved his training and knew what he wanted from you. He used to buzz off the little bits of skill I produced in training and in turn, I used to buzz off him liking those moments. That kept me going and believing. But aged 13, I could sense there were still doubts about me.

Was I going to be big enough or fill out and be able to hold my own, or would I always be considered at a disadvantage in what was a physically-biased sport at the time?

I think people could see I had the ability and, for me, it was becoming a real issue. I felt people thought I didn't have it in me to compete with the bigger lads I was facing each week when the truth is I could have held my own against anyone, the bigger the better in fact.

I had the talent and knew whoever put their faith in me would be paid back tenfold, but I was also aware there was a very real chance it might all pass me by if I didn't make a real impression at Charlton. I dug in and worked hard, making up what I lacked in inches and pounds with energy and tenacity. I just kept believing I would eventually get the breaks I needed.

We only had one pitch we trained on one evening a week and because the club recruited players from all around South and East London, there would always be way too many kids playing, but this was my best chance to impress.

We'd do a few drills, some skill-based sessions before playing a game at the end where you could hardly move for bodies. I was up against a number of kids who were 14 and 15. Everyone was kicking lumps out of each other trying to impress Roy and chief scout Les Gore who, together, would decide who they thought was worth nurturing.

You had to battle to stand out but I must have done enough as Charlton finally signed on schoolboy forms aged 14 – that gave them (and me) a year or so to see whether I was worth taking on as an apprentice. There was no way I was going to blow this chance, though I still knew there was a hell of a lot of hard work ahead of me if I was to earn an apprenticeship.

During lunchtime at school I was going in the gym and smashing weights to try and bulk up so I could fast-track the one part of my game that was missing.

I had to make the necessary sacrifices in my home and social life to try to get to where I wanted to be. I knew I needed to build my strength up because if anything was holding me back, it was my size and physique.

The one thing I'd needed was a coach who could see past my size and give me the opportunity to show exactly what I could do and in Roy, I'd found him. It was never in my DNA to give up, but I had needed something as I was ready to kick on to the next level. I'd gone from being a kid who was constantly worrying whether I'd make it or not to being one of the best players in the Charlton youth team.

I was playing right midfield as I was the youngest in the team and I can't say I was happy there because I wanted to play up front. But I was 15, still on schoolboy forms and I didn't have too much cause for complaint.

Alan Sealey was the Under-18s youth team coach while Roy, who had more of a part-time role, was in and around the club but not in charge of the teams. Alan, a former West Ham player who scored both goals in a 2-0 win the 1965 European Cup Winners' Cup final against 1860 Munich at Wembley, had the respect of the lads because he'd been there and done it.

My dad spoke of him often and told me his career had looked set to really take off after the Cup Winners' Cup but he broke his leg playing cricket with his mates a year or so later. Though made a comeback of sorts with Plymouth, he was never the same player again and after a couple of attempts to play for non-league sides, he hung his boots up aged 27.

West Ham's loss was our gain as he used his top-flight experience to great effect and was a knowledgeable and well-liked coach. Some of my team-mates included Kevin Smith, Paul Lazarus, Paul Curtis, Adrian Foley, Tony Booth, Frank Clark (not the Nottingham Forest and Newcastle Frank Clark) and Martin Ford – we were all vying for an apprenticeship.

It was an exciting time for me and a few games stick in my mind from that period, including going up to Leeds United and beating them 3-0 in the FA Youth Cup with a hat-trick from Billy Whelan.

Mark Newsome, Kevin Smith and a lad from South Africa called Richard Gough, who went on to have a fantastic career with Dundee United, Spurs, Rangers and Everton, also played.

I was playing right midfield that day and Alan gave me a bit of a bollocking afterwards for not tracking back as much as I should have done. I did work hard, but I was still prone to one or two stroppy moments if I felt I wasn't being played where I believed I should be. The problem was I liked running forwards, not going the other way! Plus I was a bit peeved that I wasn't playing up front, but it was a valuable lesson to always play the role you've been chosen for and one I never forgot.

The trip to Leeds had been the first time I'd been away representing a professional club. We travelled on a nice coach and stayed in a five-star hotel – I felt like a proper footballer and that I was really on my way. We returned home on a high and felt like our name was on the trophy already, but we drew Southampton away in the next round and lost 1-0, though we played well and gave a decent account of ourselves.

That was probably the highlight of my first season at The Valley where I was playing regularly and contributing well to the team. Alan was a great coach to me. I remember training at Chadwell Heath once and a ball came to me at 100mph and I killed it dead. Alan loved that and I know in later years he said I'd been the best kid he'd ever coached.

However, Alan left Charlton shortly afterwards following a bizarre incident involving the minibus he was ferrying us around in. I remember he clipped somebody's wing mirror but carried on driving. When we pulled up at the lights, a guy came alongside us, got out of his car holding a hammer and smashed Alan's wing mirror in.

He had to explain what had happened when he got back to the club and he left shortly afterwards – I don't know if it was connected to what had happened or not – maybe it was and he'd been skating on thin ice? I'm not sure but I was sorry to see him go.

I had no interest in a life outside football apart from girls – just a normal lad really – but I was too young to start full-time with Charlton. I'd had enough of school and I needed something to fill the void so I got myself a job through an agency (after lying about my age) and ended up working at Mattessons meat factory in East Ham, lining boxes and tins with fat while dressed from head to toe in a white overall. I did that for a month and then did odds and sods such as working at a fruit packing factory for a few weeks where I opened the crates of boxes of fruit, tipped it onto the conveyor belt and picked out the dodgy oranges. It was not the most mentally challenging work.

The thing I remember the most is the people I was working with – it was like a scene from One Flew Over the Cuckoo's Nest. They were a right bunch of doughnuts and to entertain myself, every now and then I'd throw one of the rotten oranges at the back of their heads when they had their backs turned and then quickly look as though I was busy doing something else.

They would be pissed off and looking for a fight, but though they probably knew it was me, I was always too quick and they could never actually catch me in the act. It used to keep me entertained if nothing else and I'd have a little chuckle to myself when they resumed work.

Eventually Charlton got wind of my succession of odd jobs and they told me they didn't want me working on a conveyor belt for some two-bit firm. They said I should start training – unofficially of course – with them on a full-time basis. I had to keep a low profile until I signed apprentice forms, which I did a few months later.

Secondary school seemed to fly past and to me, it was pointless continuing my education. In my final year, I hadn't been in for about six months and inevitably a guy from the school board eventually came around to see my parents. He knocked on the door and asked my mum why I hadn't been attending school.

She told him I'd just signed on at Charlton Athletic as an apprentice and was trying to become a professional footballer and he just said 'okay' and walked away. On the final day of Easter term, I went in for the last ever registration and when the teacher called my name I said, 'Yes, sir' and he looked up, smiled and just shook his head. That was where me and education went our separate ways.

The apprenticeship meant I had another two years to win a professional contract and that I'd be training with the first team every day, which is exactly what I needed. I was up against experienced pros rather than lads my own age, so I would learn more and toughen up as well.

My daily routine would include helping lay out the kit, tidying the dressing rooms, cleaning boots and all the other tasks apprentices used to have to do. I say used to because today it's nothing like that, even though I think it should be and I'm not alone in having that opinion.

After completing my tasks, I'd go training and mix in with the people I wanted to be with. I thrived in a professional environment, but I had to work hard. As an apprentice, it was our job to collect the kit after a first-team game.

The lads used to throw their shirts, shorts, socks and anything else in a pile in the middle of the dressing room for us to gather up and take to the laundry.

I remember on one occasion Lawrie Madden, one of the senior pros, threw his jockeys into the mountain of kit and it looked like there was a massive Mars Bar in them. He must have had a shit before he'd taken them off!

Derek Hales was the main man at the club back then and was known as 'Killer' to the fans – partly because of the way he played and partly because his family owned a butchers with a slaughterhouse attached to the back, where he used to work occasionally. Unluckily for Madden, Killer was the first to spot the skid-marks in his undies and he picked them up and said, 'What the fucking hell is that?'

He hung the jockeys up on a peg, mercilessly ripped into Lawrie and from then on he was known as 'Skidders' – for obvious reasons. I had a chuckle to myself but I didn't say anything at the time. Well, not immediately, anyway…

I was keeping my head down, training hard and enjoying the whole experience. Things were going well, too – better than I could have hoped, in fact. After starring for the youth team in a number of games, I made my reserve debut aged 15 away to Portsmouth in September 1978. I ran out pleased as punch at Fratton Park.

I remember the game clearly, too. It was a boiling hot afternoon on the south coast and I was playing right midfield. I had a decent game and I think Charlton boss Andy Nelson was sending a message out that if you were good enough, it didn't matter what age you were.

I vaguely recall him using me as an example to some of the older lads afterwards, telling them that here was a 15-year-old kid who had just run himself into the ground whereas one or two less motivated but more experienced players had shown a bit less desire.

It was a bit embarrassing for me, but it meant I was in the manager's mind and obviously on the right track. Everything, it seemed, was finally falling into place.

03

Breaking Good

Though I hadn't make the cut at the England Schoolboys trials, things were about to change for the better. The demoralising experience I'd had at Loughborough was soon forgotten as I finally caught the attention of the England Schoolboy scouts. During a five-a-side tournament, England youth coach John Cartwright had watched me playing and decided I had stood out, particularly the way I turned with my back to goal. I received an invite – via a letter to Charlton – to join the England youth team at a summer tournament in Yugoslavia shortly before the start of the 1979/80 season.

Shaun Brooks, Terry Gibson and Tommy Caton were some of the squad members who would later go on to make a name in senior football and I couldn't believe I was finally going to be able to pull on an England shirt. We were playing overseas in a tournament called the Adria Cup. I enjoyed training and soon felt at home among the country's most promising young talents, where I more than held my own.

I was selected to play against West Germany in the first match and I had a really good game. However, despite all my good work, my abiding memory is having a great chance to score but being denied by the keeper, who made a good save. It was my only regret, but no matter how good you are in front of goal, they don't all go in. I perhaps shouldn't have been as hard on myself as I was at the time.

The Germans were physically huge and I don't know what they'd been feeding them on but we were more than a match for them and drew 1-1. Keith James from Portsmouth had been sent off during the game and I remember him rolling around pretending to be injured, which made me laugh. While writing this book, I was saddened to hear that Keith had died in January 2015 aged just 53.

Back in Yugoslavia I was voted man-of-the-match, which was satisfying, but I knew it could have been better if I'd tucked that chance away. I set myself high standards so when things didn't go the way I wanted, I would be very self-critical.

The signs were promising though and it felt good to be among the elite group for my age. I was linking well up front with Terry Gibson who was smaller than I was, but jet-heeled.

Like me, he could also trick his way past people, so we were a handful when we were both at it. Our size, speed and mobility meant we were a bit different from the usual front pairing the opposition might have expected England to have.

We lost our next game 1-0 to Poland, but then beat Hungary

2-0 before losing 2-1 to Czechoslovakia to finish as one of the runners-up in the tournament. I'd received international recognition and made a real impression, as well as making great strides at my club in a relatively short space of time.

The tour had been thoroughly enjoyable from start to finish and I felt I'd played my part. I also noticed that my body was beginning to change. My mum mentioned when I returned home that my legs had more definition and I was finally getting the strength I had waited so long for.

The hard work was paying off, my frame was filling out and my all-round game was coming on leaps and bounds under Ian Salter, Charlton's youth team manager at the time.

I played for England Youth again later in the season against Northern Ireland at Walsall's Fellows Park and Ian came along to watch me play. I don't think I'd ever played better up to that point and without going over the top, I know I was unbelievable that night. I scored the only goal in a 1-0 win.

It was one of the most satisfying feelings I'd ever had driving back to London with Ian. He looked over at me and said, 'Well, you weren't bad, I suppose,' almost half-laughing.

He was trying to play it down a bit because the last thing they want is for you to be walking around thinking you are the bee's knees, especially aged just 16, but we both knew I was really on my way. If I kept my head down and kept working hard, more opportunities would surely come my way.

I was playing a mixture of youth and reserve team football and doing really well, but I was in a rush to get to where I wanted to be. So many lads fizzle out at that stage and are released but I never felt that would happen to me, though I didn't want to ever become complacent.

I felt I was ready to step up regardless of my age and it was generally accepted that both myself and a lad called Kevin Smith were the two most likely to move up to the first team. I'd become stronger, was more confident and I was scoring goals at both youth team and reserve team level.

In March 1979, six months after my reserve team debut, I got the call I'd been hoping for. Charlton boss Andy Nelson phoned me to say I was travelling with the senior team to Burnley in midweek and that I'd done well – though he added that this was just the start of the really hard work.

I was like a kid in a sweet shop and my mum and dad were more excited than I was, jumping up and down when I told them the news. It was a fantastic moment because this was everything I'd worked for. For a lad my age it made all the graft I'd put in at youth and reserve team level worthwhile.

I remember everything about the trip to Burnley vividly and though I didn't expect to play, I just soaked everything up. I was fascinated at the change of scenery as the coach neared the ground and the rows of terraced houses and old mills close to Turf Moor came into view.

I didn't make the bench, but I wasn't too disappointed because I knew I was in the manager's mind now. The fact I'd been included in that squad meant I would get my chance sooner or later – and as it turned out, I didn't have that long to wait.

Having being in or around the first-team squad and playing a lot in pre-season, on 22 September 1979 I made my senior Charlton debut as a sub against Shrewsbury Town. We had failed to win a single game up to that point and were bottom of the Second Division, so I think Nelson was looking for a spark from somewhere. Maybe he saw something in me that he thought might turn the tide, even though I was a few weeks shy of my 17th birthday.

There was only one sub allowed back then and I remember our captain Dick Tydeman came into the dressing room at half-time holding his groin so I knew I was going to get my chance. The gaffer told me to get warmed up because I was going on and that was when the butterflies started to flutter and the adrenaline began to really pump.

I got a fantastic round of applause from our fans as I came on for the start of the second half with the score at 1-1. I felt more than comfortable from the moment I stepped onto the pitch and things couldn't have gone much better either, as I set up what proved to be the winning goal. Tony Hazell drilled to the back post and I got up and headed the ball back across the six-yard box for Martin Robinson to score with a diving header. It was a great feeling.

Unfortunately, my parents had to miss my big day as they were away on holiday in Spain and I couldn't get hold of them to let them know, but I was waiting at the front door with a big grin on my face as they arrived back home a day or so later. I couldn't wait to tell them what had happened

With that 2-1 win we moved off the bottom of the table and I felt like I'd been injected with pure adrenaline – like an addictive drug that I immediately needed another hit of. Reserve and youth team football just couldn't compare. I played a couple more times over the next few weeks, but what I did lack was experience. I think Nelson tried to protect me by taking me out of the firing line after a couple more games.

Even though I was an inexperienced kid with just a handful of senior minutes under my belt, based on ability and potential,

I was probably one of Charlton's brightest prospects. He knew that putting too much pressure on me too soon would be detrimental. I was still raw and rough around the edges but the team already looked as though it would struggle to stay up.

As soon as I turned 17 on 1 October 1979, I went into the manager's office and told the gaffer I wanted to sign pro forms. He was more than happy to tie me to the club.

I'd been earning £12 a week plus a bit of dinner money thrown in up to that point but while I knew I'd get more, it was being able to say I was now a professional footballer that was more important. I'd only served six months of my apprenticeship, but I felt I'd earned the right to sign a deal that reflected my progress better.

I didn't have an agent so things were fairly straightforward. I took what I was offered without negotiation or question – that could all come later on. I signed a two-year contract worth £100 a week and though I knew there were some lads who were on four or five times that, the financial side of the agreement wasn't the be-all and end-all as far as I was concerned.

I was just starting out and if all the pieces fell into place, I'd get my rewards sooner rather than later. I read my contract on the bus home and kept looking at the money I'd be earning.

In effect I'd still been given a massive rise and it was a lot of money for a kid my age. As we say in South London, I was chuffed to fuck.

I was now playing occasionally for the youth team in the bigger games, playing for the reserves in midweek on a regular basis and then I would sometimes travel with the first team at the weekends. That pattern continuing over the next few months.

I was progressing all the time but Charlton weren't. We were rooted to the bottom of the old Division Two and all-but-relegated with nine games still to play. We'd lost 12 out of 14 games during a run which would, in turn, present opportunities for me to gain more valuable first-team experience.

The poor form saw Andy Nelson sacked in March 1980 and Mike Bailey take his place. I liked Andy, he'd given me my break and I was sorry to see him go, but with relegation confirmed and the pressure effectively off, Bailey looked towards the next season. He picked me in all the remaining games, none of which we won as we went from bad to worse, though I still learned a lot during them.

During the summer, I was called up for the 1980 UEFA European Youth Championships for England in East Germany. It was an interesting trip and a bit of a cultural eye-opener for me, too.

We flew into Tegel Airport and headed for Checkpoint Charlie, where I'd never really understood the political and physical divide between East and West Berlin. I knew all about the Berlin Wall, but I hadn't realised that beyond the wall there was a fence separating East and West Germany.

England physio Dave Butler told us that soldiers would be inspecting our passports and not to muck about as these were serious people. It was like something out of a war movie as a guy looked at my passport, then looked at my face, then looked back at the passport – and so on for about 30 seconds.

It was comical and because we'd been told not to laugh, it made it even harder to keep a straight face, but we all just about managed it.

We were based in Berlin overnight and you could hear marching soldiers regularly going past our hotel. It completely fascinated me – so much so that I later bought books on the subject to find out more and I wasn't really a reader at all.

I was selected to play alongside players like Mark Hateley and Tommy English, who were both already playing in Coventry City's first team, and Colin Pates and Terry Gibson were also in the side. With a lot of talented youth players to choose from, I wasn't always in the starting line-up as I'd expected to be.

I wasn't happy and was probably a bit stroppy because I was a long way from home in a hotel in Leipzig and was desperate to play. I'd been here too many times over the years and I was pretty good at letting people know I was pissed off.

I got the impression that they only wanted players who had the perfect attitude and wouldn't be disappointed that they weren't involved – but that was never going to be my mantra.

One of the England physios, Dave Butler, didn't actually say as much, but I could tell his view was that we should think we were lucky to be there. But I didn't look at it like that – far from it. I thought I deserved to play and I wasn't happy with the situation. What was the point of being there if you weren't part of it? I was never one for just making up the numbers.

We beat Northern Ireland, drew with Portugal before beating Yugoslavia, Holland and then Poland in the final. So although we won the competition, I didn't get much of a look-in apart from a couple of substitute appearances here and there. I came away with a winner's medal that I didn't feel I'd earned.

We returned home and though the rest of the lads were in celebratory mood, I was frustrated at not having played a bigger part during the tournament.

I turned my thoughts to what I hoped would be a better season with Charlton as the 1980/81 season loomed, but I didn't get off to the best of starts. I'd returned home from my England trip a bit flat but within a few weeks I was setting off again for a pre-season tour of Sweden with Charlton. It was there I got into a bit of bother when I was caught by a member of the backroom staff with a local girl in my room.

Mike Bailey was quite hard-nosed, but fair and he didn't take any nonsense. He'd already doubled my wages to £200 a week so my timing could have been a lot better.

He'd recently received a letter from England Youth suggesting that my attitude at the tournament wasn't all that it should have been and after I'd been summoned to see him, he read the letter out verbatim, underlining that, for him, this was my second hint of an attitude problem in the space of a few weeks.

I think he was just reminding me of where I was and how I was expected to behave for my club and country – which he was entitled to do. It was the right thing because although I didn't feel as though I was getting carried away, it didn't do any harm to give me a bit of a bollocking every now and then just to keep my feet firmly planted on the ground.

Meanwhile, training with the likes Derek Hales, Dick Tydeman, Colin Powell, Martin Robinson, Steve Gritt, Lawrie Madden and Phil Warman was really bringing my game on.

I'd reached as far as I could go at youth level and needed better opposition and though Bailey had expressed his displeasure at my behaviour, he didn't drop me. I played in all the pre-season games and had also started to forge a decent understanding with Addicks legend Derek Hales up front.

'Killer' was the leader in the dressing room and there was an opportunity to fill the sizeable void left by Mike Flanagan, who had moved on to Crystal Palace for big money. Flanagan had been Hales' striker partner for several seasons but their relationship had deteriorated after fighting on the pitch during a cup match with Maidstone.

The resentment had been simmering for a while and it finally come to a head with a moment that did little for either the club or the players involved. I think Flanagan felt he'd been the better player in what had been a prolific partnership, but maybe didn't like the fact Hales was more popular with the supporters. Having said that, there were all sorts of rumours flying around as to why they didn't like each other.

That ill-feeling between them finally bubbled to the surface with Hales sticking a few punches on Flanagan. They both ended up being bizarrely sent off with the rest of the players and our fans watching on bemused. It carried on in the dressing room until they were separated, with Flan mostly exonerated of blame. Hales was initially sacked but later reinstated.

The only way forward was for one of them to leave and so Flan moving on created an opportunity for me – I doubt I'd have been given a chance as I early as I had if Flanagan and Hales had still been knocking the goals in regularly.

I was still a bit green around the gills as we began the 1980/81 season in Division Three (now League One). Aged 17 as we kicked off the campaign, I knew if I started well, I'd have a good chance of establishing myself in the first team.

Bizarrely, we would start off with three South London derbies against Brentford, two of which were League Cup ties. It was in the first leg away to Brentford that I scored my first goal for Charlton and though we lost 3-1, it was a great feeling to get off the mark. There was more to come thought and four days later in the second leg, I really announced my arrival.

We beat Brentford 5-0 at The Valley and I scored a hat-trick, becoming the youngest player in the club's history to achieve that feat.

It took me a bit longer to get my first league goal, which had become something of an issue for me, but once I finally broke my duck, a weight was lifted. I didn't look back and I would score 18 goals in all competitions that season, with Derek Hales scoring more than 20, and I ended up in the PFA Third Division Team of the Year.

One game that sticks in my mind from that season was when we played at home to Blackpool where my boyhood hero Alan Ball, then aged 36, was player-manager. I couldn't believe I was actually playing against Bally and even better, I scored the winning goal in a 2-1 win.

As we were walking off, I looked round to see where he was and he was behind me, about to put his arm around my shoulder. He said, in his unmistakably high-pitched voice, 'Hey young fella, if you keep working you might be a player one day.'

He did an interview after the game and said that if a player was good enough, he was old enough for the England team. I'll never forget him backing me like that and our paths would cross again in the future, with mixed fortunes for both of us.

Bally's glowing reference didn't do my confidence any harm and I think Mike Bailey might have thought I was a bit too big for my boots at times and maybe a bit too sure of myself, but I never felt I was too cocky. I was confident and never fazed by anything – the bottom line was I believed I deserved my place in the team and I think my goals backed that up.

I was playing my part by making and scoring goals and I always worked hard because it was in my nature to play that way. However, despite your best intentions, I suppose it's easy to get carried away every now and then so when my comeuppance finally came, I'd been heading towards it for a while.

We'd been having a game of keepy-uppy while waiting for the team photo to be taken at the training ground and as I flicked the ball to Lawrie Madden, he miscontrolled it and the ball bounced away. I sighed and, remembering the Mars Bar and Killer's nickname for him, I said, 'Ah, come on Skidders...'

A few of the lads were chuckling to themselves but he glared at me and said, 'You fucking call me Skidders one more time and I'll give you a fucking whack.'

I said, 'Oh yeah, good story,' and we carried on juggling the ball. Inevitably, a few minutes later the juggling ended with Madden again and I couldn't help myself. 'For fuck's sake Skidders!'

With that he came straight for me, told me to fuck off and punched square on the nose, breaking it in the process. I wasn't having that. I jumped on top of him, trying to whack him back and suddenly my nose just started gushing blood everywhere and we separated.

I went back into the dressing room and was lying on the treatment table with an icepack on my nose when Mike Bailey came in to see what had happened. I could detect a look of pleasure in his eyes as if to say, 'Thank fuck someone has finally given him a dig.'

He probably thought it might quieten me down a bit. At least, that's what I read into it and even though I wasn't best pleased at the time, looking back, it was pretty funny.

I was comfortable enough to be myself with other lads and there was never any malice in me, I was just chirpy and enjoyed the banter. But from Madden's point of view, he couldn't be seen to have the piss taken out of him by a kid nearly eight years his junior. I suppose I'd been asking for a clip – as I say, the gaffer probably thought I'd had it coming and maybe he was right.

The one good thing about the whole incident was that I'd stood up for myself and had been on him in a shot. In a strange way, Madden and the rest of the lads knew that they couldn't take the piss out of me and things went back to normal after that, with no hard feelings between us.

Back on the pitch, we had been top of the table from November to April and even got as far as the fifth round of the FA Cup where we faced Bobby Robson's Ipswich Town at Portman Road. We must have taken 5,000 fans with us to Suffolk and were up against one of the best teams in the country, with Ipswich challenging Liverpool for the title at the time.

Two divisions beneath them, we were the lowest ranked team still left in the competition.

We gave a good account of ourselves but were up against a team that included Arnold Muhren, Frans Thijssen, George Burley, Mick Mills, Alan Brazil, John Wark, Eric Gates and Kevin Beattie and we were beaten 2-0. Ipswich went on to the semis where they were beaten by Manchester City, who in turn would lose to Spurs in the final.

It was a great experience and the first 'proper' game against quality opposition I can remember. Even though we'd had friendlies against West Ham and other top sides, this had been the real thing.

Back in the league, we did our best to blow promotion, winning just two of 11 games between the end of February and mid-April before finally securing our spot at Carlisle United, who had Peter Beardsley playing for them at the time. I scored in a 3-1 win and we were back in Division Two (now the Championship) again.

It had been a great season, one that I'd thoroughly enjoyed and felt I'd played my part to the full. I was voted Charlton Athletic's Young Player of the Year and I'd become quite popular with the supporters, who even had their own song for me: 'We all agree, Paul Walsh is magic'. Okay, not a classic but I loved it.

I couldn't have asked for a better first full season. I knew people would be wondering whether I could cut it at a higher level. I'd need to do the same and more if I was to get to where I wanted to be the following year, but I was confident I would kick on.

I was an England Youth regular by this point and having proved I could hold my own at senior level, there were rumours in the papers that several bigger clubs were already keeping an eye on me. I used to love reading the transfer gossip columns in the Sunday papers and I remember one time being linked with Manchester United, Manchester City, Aston Villa and Everton in the News of the World.

It was everything I'd ever dreamed of. I was still a teenager and it didn't matter if it wasn't true – I enjoyed showing my dad and some of the other lads well, even if it was just to wind them up a bit. We had a good group of players and we'd taken the club back up at the first attempt, so there was plenty of optimism around the place, though the 1981/82 season would see major changes that would affect the club's future – and mine.

04

Mad Hatter

While my first full season had caught the eye of a number of bigger clubs, I wasn't the only person at Charlton who had attracted interest on the back of a successful campaign. Mike Bailey had steered us to promotion and, as a result, he was offered the vacant post at Brighton and Hove Albion – a position he understandably accepted. Alan Mullery had lost his job at the Goldstone Ground and ironically, he replaced Bailey at Charlton. Along with his assistant Ken Craggs, we had a new management team.

It was all change again and, in only my second full season in the first team, I was already playing under my third manager. I would have to impress a new man all over again. Mullery wasted no time strengthening the team for the campaign ahead and brought in some experienced players such as Don McAllister and Terry Naylor from Spurs plus Leighton Phillips from Swansea City and Chelsea keeper John Phillips.

Along with some of the players we already had like Nicky Johns, Kevin Smith and Paul Elliott, we were at best a solid mid-table with aspirations of an outside promotion bid. I'd never really had many dealings with our chairman Michael Gliksten before but, from what I'd heard, he seemed like a decent fella.

Suddenly he was gone and replaced with a new guy called Mark Hulyer, who turned up and was very hands-on with his approach – a bit too much for the lads' liking.

I didn't know if he was the new chairman or if he'd bought the club outright, but word quickly got round that he was now the main man.

He started travelling to games on the team coach, which is a bit of an inner sanctum to the players, and he soon took a particular liking to me and seemed keen to get to know me better. He invited me around to his house and asked me to bring my scrapbooks with me. I didn't see any harm in it and thought no more of it.

It proved to be a bit of a rollercoaster campaign and after ten games we were looking good in fifth place – then we lost five of our next six matches and dropped a dozen places. But we'd yo-yo our way through the year and lost just one of our next 14 to move up to seventh.

Going into March, we were tipped as dark horses for promotion. Those hopes soon went up in smoke as we won just one of our final 11 games, losing eight and scoring only six goals to finish smack bang in mid-table.

I'd had a decent season and scored maybe 15 goals in total –

not as many as my first season – but we'd done okay and the bottom line was we'd held our own in a tougher division.

I remember finishing the season feeling a bit frustrated at how things had ended and Mullery walking over to me outside The Valley as I got in my car. I nodded and kept my door open as he drew closer. He said, 'Look, you've got to get away from here, kid.'

I think he could see where the club was heading financially and the penny started to drop that Mark Hulyer's real interest in me was because I was probably the only player he could get some real money for. At that time, Charlton were desperate for an influx of cash.

It was just business I suppose and I didn't think too much more about it. Instead I just enjoyed the summer break the same way any 19-year-old would. I remember I was lying in bed having had a few late nights with some of my mates and my mum came knocking on my door.

I woke up eventually and she said, 'There's some bloke called David Pleat on the phone for you, love.' I knew who he was so I went down and took the call, wondering what it was all about but half sussing what he was about to say.

I picked up the phone. 'Hello Paul, David Pleat the Luton Town manager here. Just thought I'd call to let you know that we'd like to sign you and wondered whether or not you'd like to come and play for us?'

He said I'd impressed him over the previous couple of seasons when Charlton had played Luton in the league and enjoyed watching me have a rare old tussle with one of his trusted lieutenants, Mal Donaghy, who was someone he really rated.

I think we only scored one goal in those four games so I must have done something other than scoring goals to impress Pleat! It was a lot to take in and I was a bit surprised but said, 'Yeah, sure, I'd love to.' We spoke a bit more and I put the phone down and tried to absorb the conversation I'd just had.

I had to wait a few days before the club informed me officially they'd accepted Luton's offer of £400,000 for me plus Steve White, who'd scored 30 goals for them on the way to promotion to Division One that season.

Disappointingly, the chairman made it clear to me that he'd make my life difficult if the deal didn't go through so I felt a little pressured into agreeing to the move. Although I'd have more than likely gone anyway, it would have been nice to feel that I had a choice in the matter.

I'd regularly been linked with Everton, Aston Villa and Manchester United over the summer and, if I'm honest, Luton Town was a little disappointing in comparison to huge clubs of that size. Still, it was a good opportunity for me to kick on and it represented a step up from where I was.

The fact was, if there had been any other offers – bigger offers – Charlton would have bitten their hands off, but maybe I was still seen as unproven in the top flight and therefore a bit of a gamble at the price I was being valued at.

I called my team-mate Leighton Phillips to ask a bit of advice. Phillips said I should go for it and put a few numbers in my mind for when terms were discussed, though he thought a bigger club would come in for me at some point.

A meeting was arranged at The Ritz in Mayfair, where a suite had been hired to finalise the deal. Hulyer was there, as was Ken Craggs, who was by then the new Charlton manager following Mullery's departure (no surprise after our car park chat) plus

David Pleat and little old me, aged 19. There had been talk that I was on the verge of being included in Ron Greenwood's full England squad as well, so things were really taking off for me and I felt I had a decent bargaining position to get a good deal.

Luton had hired a plush suite with a large lounge and bedroom off to the side and another smaller room opposite. After the small talk, we finally got around to talking about what sort of money I was looking for. I had no representation and no experience of situations like that, so I started spouting some of the numbers Leighton Phillips had suggested I ask for.

After a while, Pleat suggested I should go and wait in the smaller side room while everyone had a little chat. Looking back, I think the only real number done was one on me! I was sat in the next room with the door open (accidentally on purpose from their point of view) and they were probably more than aware I could hear everything that was being said.

I heard someone say, 'Christ, he's asking for telephone numbers here,' and I started to think that maybe I had asked for too much but, looking back, it was just a game they were playing. I'm sure the 'confidential' discussion they were having was with broad smiles on their faces as I was set up to accept a lower amount.

The offer was indeed less than I'd asked for, but it was still respectable and a lot more than I'd been on at Charlton. There was a basic wage, appearance money, signing-on fee and other incentives that made it up to be a nice package. I agreed terms and was fairly happy with the deal.

There was one slightly awkward side to the transfer, however. Steve White had also been invited to the hotel but he had no idea why. There were a number of interconnecting doors in the suite and I had to go into the bedroom when Steve arrived. Then I came out when he'd been shown into another room, where he was asked to wait until he was called. It was ridiculous and a bit hard on him, but Luton had to be sure I was signing before they could hit him with the bombshell that Charlton wanted him to move in the other direction.

Once I'd agreed, I left the room and Steve was invited in. I know he was really disappointed when he found out Luton were prepared to sell him. After the season he'd had, I could understand him being gutted but once he realised he wasn't wanted at Kenilworth Road, I think he resigned himself to moving.

There were a few things to iron out and I'd pen the contract a few days later. I wasn't sure whether it was good business for Charlton and I know a lot of the supporters felt I'd been sold on the cheap.

Maybe they were right – but my time at The Valley was now at an end and the club banked £400,000 for a player who hadn't cost them a penny – most of which they spent on former European Footballer of the Year Allan Simonsen. He would play just 16 games before moving on three months later with the club unable to pay his wages.

I loved my time with Charlton and had even turned down the chance to train with my boyhood team Arsenal to join them in the first place. I'd learned so much while I'd been with the club and had some great coaches who had helped bring my game on. I'd been given a chance early on to make an impression and I'd enjoyed the pressure, the politics of whether I'd make it or not.

I had travelled around Europe with the youth team and loved every minute of it. The cold truth is Charlton were a vehicle for me and I was a commodity to them. I could dress it up and say I was heartbroken to move on, but it wouldn't be true.

If I'd not been good enough, they'd have shown me the door so everything I achieved there I had to earn – nothing in life comes for free. The fans had been fantastic towards me and I still remember the first time I heard them sing my name. Anyone who thinks I don't have a great appreciation for the club couldn't be more wrong.

Today, I think a one or two Charlton fans are under the impression that I hold no affection for the club. The truth is I played for them a long time ago – more than 30 years ago in fact – but my time there will always mean a lot to me.

I still enjoy going back to The Valley, but there is one thing that really bugs me. I actually find it a bit sad that they have all these pictures of former players on the walls but you have to walk a long way to find mine, which is tucked away in a bar near the toilets.

However, there is one of Allan Simonsen, who was at the club for all of five minutes and was bought with most of the money the club got for me.

I went on to play in a European Cup final, win the league, FA Cup and League Cup. There can't be too many Charlton youth team players who went on to do that, so I hope the fans got some pleasure from seeing me progress to bigger and better things as time went on. They will always be the club who gave me my break and set me on my way.

Over at Kenilworth Road, I had to attend the press conference with David Pleat to announce the deal was done and that I was now a Luton Town player. There were local media and some national journalists in attendance as well. Luton is in a decent catchment area for coverage with Anglia TV, Central TV and London all covering the club back then.

Brian Stein was also part of the press conference, but from the very first time I met him, I sensed there was a little something there that wasn't quite right.

It wasn't the most friendly welcome I'd ever had and maybe there was a bit of resentment that I'd come in. Steve White had gone despite scoring so many goals and helping Luton win promotion – I couldn't put my finger on it, but I didn't feel he was exactly embracing the fact that I was going to be his new striker partner.

Pleat maybe sensed that too and gambled by deciding we should room together for the upcoming season – if we were going to gel, we needed to get on and get to know each other both on and off the pitch.

Gradually, things got better and during a pre-season tour of Sweden, we found ourselves in a place called Eskilstuna. It was a great laugh from start to finish, there was a real camaraderie among the lads and I was quickly accepted as part of the squad.

I was able to relax and really enjoy myself and all I wanted to do really was settle in and get to know the lads.

I wanted to integrate myself as quickly as possible and we trained hard, played hard but made sure we enjoyed ourselves at night. I was getting along better with Steiny as well and sensed a thaw in the initial frostiness.

I remember one night when we went out and as the evening wore on, I got talking to a local girl who ended up coming back to the training camp with me. I didn't have a key to the front door and so looked alongside the building for a way to get in.

There was a line of windows with the ground falling away

the further you went along. Only one window was open, so we headed for that. I lifted her up to get in, then she helped me clamber up as well. So we were both in the room, not knowing where we were, but keen to find my room.

I walked over to the door to figure out where I was, just as it opened and in walked David Pleat – of all the rooms to climb into, I'd picked the gaffer's! He looked suitably confused and said, 'What are you both doing? Where are you going?'

I had to think quickly and said, 'I'm going to bed, we've got training in the morning,' and walked out. Safe to say I never saw the girl again. She followed me out of the room and quickly left the building via the front door, with me walking in the opposite direction, ever the gentleman!

The next morning all the lads were talking about it. One of the coaches told me Pleaty hadn't known what to do with his new striker appearing in his bedroom at night then acting as though everything was normal. It had turned out to be an inspired decision to play dumb.

I was enjoying myself and really hit it off with one of my new team-mates, Wayne Turner, somebody who would become a lifelong friend and partner in crime. He was a midfielder who was just a couple of years older than me and also a local lad from Luton. We got on like a house on fire.

On another night out on tour, a few of us ended up back at a flat with some local girls after partying in a few bars. The women were a bit older than we were and Wayne and I weren't that interested, but we still enjoyed ourselves.

In the corner there was an old rocking horse that looked like some sort of family heirloom, but it was about to bite the dust because it completely disintegrated when Wayne sat on it. We proceeded to mess about, using the broken pieces of the horse as instruments and just generally being a pain in the arse.

We were just young, single lads enjoying ourselves but eventually the night fizzled out and we headed back to the hotel.

On the way back, we had to cross a deserted dual carriageway and it was at that point that Wayne decided he needed a shit – so he took one in the middle of the road. His work of art looked like a Walnut Whip with a little signature peak at the top. His nickname ever since has been, predictably, 'Whip'.

By the time we came home I felt completely at ease, one of the lads and was ready for my first season at Kenilworth Road, though I still had a few personal loose ends to tie up.

I still went out with my mates in my old neighbourhood whenever I could as they were good levellers and we always had great banter. We drank in an area that was part Millwall and part Charlton so there was the odd occasion when things almost got out of hand. By in large, I managed to steer clear of bother – though there was the odd exception.

I was a lively lad, as were my mates, and you knew when we were around. We probably got on people's nerves from time to time. We were drinking in a regular haunt of ours, the Jolly Drayman, and we sometimes pushed things a bit too far I suppose. Every now and then we upset one or two punters.

We were always on the edge with our wind-ups and our verbals sometimes didn't go down that well. We were young and dressed smartly, so we were quite popular with the girls. Because I was doing well as a footballer, it was inevitable that I would end up a target for a bit of payback every now and then.

One night, I popped in for a quick pint at the Drayman and when I left, I didn't realise I had company. I was about to get in my car when I noticed two blokes approaching me out of the corner of my eye. I sensed immediately something wasn't right but was wary enough that, when they drew closer, I managed to duck as one of them took a swing at me.

I then set off running up the street because I didn't fancy my chances against two of them. Of course, being the early Eighties, the clothes I was wearing didn't help my escape. My leather shoes and tight jeans made it awkward because I kept slipping as I ran – the price of being fashionable!

But I was fit as a fiddle and soon put distance between me and them. I looked back down the road and while one of the guys had conked out after a few yards, the other was still chasing after me.

So I had a think and decided to wait for him to catch up. When he got to me he was so fucked he couldn't even raise his fists, so I did the decent thing and beat the shit out of him.

Those sort of situations were making it a bit uncomfortable to go out in a group and I started to watch over my shoulder a bit more. In truth, the move away from the area came at just about the right time for me, as sooner or later we'd have ended up in trouble.

I'd bought a two-bed flat in Sidcup for £29,000 not long before I joined Luton and though it wasn't furnished, it was mine and it was great to feel that I had a bit of independence if I needed it. My mum was particularly upset that I'd finally flown the nest and she was crying her eyes out when I eventually moved out of the family home, but she understood it was time to spread my wings.

The thing was, I never really moved into my bachelor pad as it wasn't going to be much use now I was at Luton some 40 miles away. I mentioned to Pleaty that I was thinking of selling it and buying one in Luton instead, but he advised me to give digs a go and hold off buying another place.

He said that I'd have company on some nights when I needed it, everything would be done for me and there would be someone to keep an eye on me. I was reluctant to try it, but on his advice I gave it a go and as it turned out, he was spot-on. I moved in with an older girl called Madge who lived just outside Luton.

She had a lorry driver son called Barry who was in his mid-forties and was there every now and then. I'd eat with them, talk to them and they were good company, but I still had my own life as well.

I'd nip out on Thursdays to play snooker and on Friday's I'd either be away with the team or tucked up in bed at a reasonable time before a game. It was cheap as chips and I would stay with the family throughout my time with Luton. They were great people who I really enjoyed my time with.

I started my Luton career with a 2-2 draw away to Spurs at White Hart Lane. We were up against a side that included Steve Archibald, Garth Crooks and Glenn Hoddle among others, but we still came away a decent result.

It was a glimpse of what was to come as we more than held our own in the early months of the campaign. The goals were flying in from all angles, but my home debut against West Ham should have gone better than it actually did.

I missed a great chance to score a goal at 0-0 and I knew I should have done better. We went on to lose 2-0, but if the fans were wondering whether the club had been right to shell out the money on me, a few days later against Notts County, I announced my top-flight arrival in style and hopefully allayed any fears. It was a cracking game and I scored my first before the break, but my second remains one of the best goals I ever scored. I picked the ball up on the right, rode one challenge as I entered the box before cutting inside another defender and lifting the ball past the keeper.

It was later voted Goal of the Season and when I watch old clips of the goal on YouTube, the hairs on my neck still stand up as I watch the celebration afterwards. Not long after David Moss broke clear on the right, sent in a low cross and I prodded home my third, completing my hat-trick in what eventually ended up with us winning 5-3 win.

I was absolutely buzzing and 'There's only one Paul Walsh!' was echoing around Kenilworth Road towards the end of the game – something I'll never forget on what had been a brilliant day for me.

05

Mission Impossible

It's fair to say that the football Luton were playing was a breath of fresh air. The club received praise from all quarters for the all-out attacking philosophy David Pleat encouraged us to play. We were scoring goals for fun but shipping way too many as well. Inevitably there were some crazy scores along the way. It was fantastic for a player like me because I had been given so much freedom. We were all encouraged to express ourselves and play with instinct, which was perfect for me and a number of other like-minded lads in the team.

We followed the 5-3 win over Notts County with a 4-1 defeat away to Aston Villa and then drew 3-3 away to Liverpool which, unbeknown to me at the time, was a match that would also help shape my future career.

WALSHY

I'd grown up watching Liverpool's midweek European nights on TV and, like many others at that time, I had a soft spot for the club. There was an aura about Anfield and the traditions the club had set it apart for a number of years.

Kevin Keegan and John Toshack, Bill Shankly, the Kop singing You'll Never Walk Alone swaying back and forth – there was something really special about the club. And here I was at Anfield, actually playing in front of that same Kop.

I was up against Mark Lawrenson on the day. He was at the peak of his powers and part of the best defence in England by a mile. But I was about to give him an afternoon to forget and also ensure it wasn't just the supporters who went home remembering my name.

I picked up the ball in my own half, skipped past one challenge and headed for the left-hand side of the Liverpool box as Lawrenson closed in. I knew I couldn't outpace him so I made him think I was turning into him and didn't know what I was doing. As he thought he had the ball, I lifted it over his foot and raced into the box, leaving him for dead.

I squared it to Brian Stein who had plenty to do, but he made it look easy as he finished with a sidefoot shot into the top corner to give Bruce Grobbelaar no chance. I'd proved I could take on the best and beat them, but what I didn't realise was that I'd planted a seed in the mind of Liverpool boss Bob Paisley, who would start to take an interest in my progress.

It was a memorable game for a number of reasons, not least that we had three different keepers during the 90 minutes. First of all our regular keeper Jake Findlay threw the ball out and then went down injured as though he'd been hit by a sniper, so defender Kirk Stevens went in goal. He stayed in until half-time when Mal Donaghy took over but at 3-2, we were still right in the game. When the ball fell to David Moss, he made it 3-3 with a brilliant strike with the outside of his boot to earn us a draw few people had given us any chance of getting.

We'd shown no fear in Liverpool's own backyard and maybe taken them by surprise, as not many teams attacked them the way we'd done. It was further proof that, on our day, we could score goals against anyone, home or away. We left Anfield cock-a-hoop and enjoyed the trip back south.

The goals kept flowing. We beat Brighton 5-0 before drawing 4-4 with Stoke City at The Victoria Ground – a total of 38 goals scored and conceded in just seven games meant we'd announced our arrival on the big stage in style. However, there was no way we could sustain that ratio and if the goals scored dried up, we'd be in trouble.

Part of the reason we were doing so well was Pleaty's No.2, David Coates, who was a great coach and a really positive guy to have around because he only saw the good in everything. He used to take Steiny and me for extra shooting sessions along with keeper Les Sealey.

If you scored against Les, he took it badly and all you'd hear was him muttering 'fuck!' or 'cunt!' under his breath every time the ball nestled in the back of his net. Steiny and I loved to beat him and wind him up with the occasional, 'Come on – you should've got that one, Les,' to which you were guaranteed a 'fuck off!' in return. Steiny and I would take the piss and it would be hilarious, as it was so easy to push his buttons.

Luton had become the neutral's favourites and my performances in the first few weeks earned me my first England Under-21 call-up. Dave Sexton and Howard Wilkinson shared the England Under-21 coaching role at the time and though I'd been on their radar at Charlton, I think my hat-trick against Notts County probably convinced them I was worth a place in the team.

Mark Hateley and Tommy English were still blocking my path as they had been a few years earlier in the youth team, mainly because they had been regulars for Coventry in the top flight for a couple of years, but I eventually established myself as one of the first choice strikers at Under-21 level during that season.

We had a good side, with my club team-mate Brian Stein – who was in the squad as one of the permitted over-age players – Stoke City's Mark Chamberlain, Arsenal midfielder Paul Davis, Hateley and English, Chelsea's Colin Pates, Tommy Caton from Manchester City, Watford pair Nigel Callaghan and John Barnes plus Everton's Steve McMahon among others.

We had so much talent coming through at once and there was real reason for optimism that England could be a force again at international level in future years. If I kept my head down and continued to play as I had been doing, there was no reason why I couldn't be part of it all.

I was under the impression that me and Barnsey were the two manager Bobby Robson was looking at more closely to elevate to the senior squad, so everything was looking rosy.

I made my England Under-21 debut as a sub, coming on for Paul Bracewell during a 4-1 win over Denmark in September 1982 with Howard Wilkinson in charge on the night. I tried not to let any of it go to my head, which would have been easy as a 19-year-old with so much going for me, but my confidence had never been higher.

After the incident in the Jolly Drayman car park a few months earlier where I'd been targeted for a thumping, I kept my feet on the ground as best I could and was a lot more aware when I did go out socialising than maybe I had been before.

I'd taken on Bev Walker as my agent by that point, the same guy who represented Arsenal's Charlie Nicholas. Charlie had made his name with Celtic and had been getting a lot of attention up in Scotland, where he was becoming a big star both on and off the pitch. However that probably trebled when he moved down to London.

Bev got me and Charlie to take part in a photoshoot together in London where we both had guns for the old sharp-shooters line – the usual corny stuff. Not long after he said he'd got a sponsorship deal for us both, which meant we'd each get a car.

It's funny how you trust your agent to the point you don't even read the paperwork, but I wish I had, because it turned out he'd got us to sign a HP agreement for the car. Charlie and I were paying for the cars we thought were sponsored and free!

Bev was simply adding the cost to his bill and though I'd got a few little deals here and there with shinpads, boots and the like, when I saw the invoice he'd sent me, I saw that I actually owed him money. So much for the sponsorship! That was the end of that as far as Bev was concerned.

Still, Charlie and I had a nice Mitsubishi Starion each – a decent car for a kid my age, though it was a bit flash and nothing more than a poor man's Ferrari.

I suppose I was a bit of a rascal at that time in that I was young, free and single, as was Wayne Turner, so we had some good laughs. Nobody was safe from our piss-taking when we were together. The worst thing Luton could have done was tie up a sponsorship deal with brewery giants Whitbread, because part of the agreement was that every now and then two players would pair up and go to different pubs around Luton to meet the supporters while having a few beers with them.

It might have seemed like a good idea on paper, but that's as far as it should have gone. I was sent with Brian Stein to a pub called The Studio, but it was the sort of place a young footballer should have stayed well away from. It was dark, had a young crowd, lots of pretty girls and good music, placing temptation squarely on a plate in front of us.

I was also a bit wary of going out and meeting the fans because Wayne had an uneasy relationship with a small group of our supporters, probably for no other reason than he was a local lad made good.

While they loved the fact we played for Luton and were helping the team establish itself in the top flight, there was an element of resentment towards us because we had money and always had a load of girls around us.

That said, there was an incident a few months earlier that hadn't exactly endeared us to a few of local idiots. We'd won 3-2 away to Birmingham City in October 1982 and I'd scored the winning goal. We headed home in high spirits and Wayne and I were keen to get out and celebrate the win.

We'd moved up to eighth in the table and went out to The Studio for a few beers. Mick Carroll ran the place and he had become good friends with both me and Wayne, which in turn meant we could do pretty much whatever we wanted in there.

There were big TV screens everywhere and Match of the Day was on in the background when we arrived. Wayne and I were sat at the bar having a few drinks and a few girls had inevitably gravitated around us. I recognised a hardcore group of Luton fans who were watching the match on the screens. They kept glancing over at me and Wayne and muttering comments to each other.

You didn't have to be a rocket scientist to work out what they were thinking. As they gradually got more pissed they became more agitated. I'd put a fair amount of money on them saying something like, 'Yeah, they're playing for our team but look at them. Flash cunts.'

In jest and to show I wasn't bothered about what they thought of us, I half-raised my glass towards them, winding them up a bit more, but only as a laugh. It was perfect timing because it was around that time that Luton's game was on the big screens.

I watched as I was put clean through on goal and as the keeper came out I put it through his legs and wheeled away celebrating. But there was no cheering in the bar – far from it as a few of the lads, already pissed and pissed off at us, threw their pints at the big screens and looked over to see our reaction.

In for a penny – we raised our glasses again as if to say 'cheers lads!' We were probably lucky it didn't develop into something more serious, but I wasn't going to be intimidated by anybody, especially as I was only enjoying myself and nothing more.

While I'd come out of one or two scrapes quite well during my Luton days, there was one occasion where I actually managed to stay out of a fight but ended up having to be bailed out at 4am in the morning by David Pleat.

A few of my mates had come up to Luton for a night out – Doug Colville, David Gilligan, Steven Middleton – and they were all smartly dressed, as they always were to be fair. We were heading out with Wayne to a nightclub called Cinderella Rockefellers, which was a place where we almost always had a problem of some kind. Most places in the area welcomed minor celebrities and footballers with open arms and the DJ loved us there and we always enjoyed ourselves.

On this particular night we were in the queue waiting to go in. Wayne and I had a nickname for the head doorman which was 'FA Cup Head' on account of his massive ears. He hated us and we were always giving him stick so he was most likely looking for a reason to get a bit of payback. This time, he got it.

The dress-code was that you had to wear a tie and it didn't matter if you were the scruffiest man in the world – if you wore a tie you'd get it. Two of the lads had ties on and looked a million dollars while Doug looked really smart wearing a cashmere jacket and expensive shirt, trousers and shoes. As we were about to go in, FA Cup Head said, 'No, no, you're not coming in' to Doug.

I said, 'Leave it out mate,' just as this toe-rag who looked like he lived on the street – but was wearing a tie – was allowed to walk past us and into the club.

We were waiting at the side, complaining as a succession of blokes were let in and the lads had seen enough. Steve was a bit of an amateur boxer, Gilly was up for anything and Doug was also in the mix but I thought I needed to keep out of it. Things were starting to take off with my career so the last thing I could afford was to get mixed up in anything.

Doug went to push one of the bouncers out of the way and it just kicked off from there. There were haymakers flying around in the reception area, people rolling around but I needed to keep out of it so I stepped out of the door. I kept trying to peek in to see what was going on, but there was a another bouncer watching me and I knew the moment I stepped in, there'd be no going back. I pushed the door again so it opened and I could see what was happening but the bouncer pushed it back at me – I tried to kick it back open with my foot and as I did, I cracked the tiniest pane of reinforced glass you've ever seen at the bottom of the door.

Things calmed down and we were ready to move on when a police van turned up and threw us all in. The bouncers identified us and we were taken to a police station in Dunstable where we all had our trousers and shoes taken off us as evidence and then we were put in a cell for the night. They'd also taken my little address book, but there wasn't anything we could do so I settled down for the night.

About 4am, the slide went back on the door and a voice said, 'There's someone to see you.' The door opened and it was David Pleat – they must have rung him up – and he had what I took to be a wry smile as he looked at me sitting there in my shirt, socks and undies. He'd bailed me out and he went to get a blanket from his car.

My mates stayed locked up all night but I was in bed by about 5am. I was charged with criminal damage and received a fine but the worst part of it all was that it story was reported in several papers so it wasn't the smartest thing I'd ever done, even though I hadn't really done anything!

So there were one or two incidents, but no more than that, and it wasn't going to stop us doing what we wanted to do. Wayne had it worse than me and he was always being picked on by somebody or other, but he batted it off quite well.

Luton was a decent place, but there was definitely a small-town mentality among some of the lads of a similar age.

I was living the bachelor life, enjoying myself and had no ties, but that was about to change during my first season with the Hatters when I met a girl who I began to go out with.

All the lads socialised after a home game and we enjoyed other's company. We'd have a few drinks and sometimes go on for a meal. There were plenty of bars in and around the ground to choose from as a starting point.

After one game, we all met up as usual. But I'd picked up a knee injury that was giving me a lot of pain so I thought the alcohol might ease the discomfort a little – as you do! The club doctor Bill Berry and his wife Pat were in the bar, as was their very attractive daughter Melissa. After a couple of beers I plucked up enough courage to ask if she'd like to come out a for a few drinks.

She very politely declined and I thought no more about it. I left Kenilworth Road and drove down Oak Road, which is full of potholes and bumps. The car behind appeared to be flashing me for some reason, so I pulled over to find out what the problem was.

As I got closer I could see it was the doc and his wife and as they drew alongside, Melissa jumped out and got in my front seat. I suppose fate was playing a hand because the doc hadn't been flashing his lights, they were just dipping every time he went over a bump, but Melissa had made up her mind that she would come out after all.

I had my leg in a big bandage but I could still drive okay. We ended up going to a nightclub and having a great night out, though I couldn't move around too well. We enjoyed each other's company and the only problem was I needed to get her home to Stevenage 15 miles or so away. I was worse for wear, having had a few drinks over the course of the night. I'm a ashamed to say I drove back fairly pissed, which I know was very irresponsible.

When we arrived at her parents house, Melissa's dad took one look at me and told me to come in and get some sleep in the spare room. In the morning Bill made me breakfast and told me in a nice way that I shouldn't be driving around when I'd had that much to drink, especially with his daughter as a passenger. Suitably chastised, I drove home, but it was the beginning of a long-term relationship with Melissa.

Back on the pitch and things had taken a turn for the worse. We'd gone eight games without winning after the Birmingham victory and by New Year we'd won just twice in 13 and had slipped down to 18th place.

There was plenty of time to put things right and we had a great squad with the skipper Brian Horton, David Moss, Brian Stein, Mal Donaghy, Raddy Antic and Kirk Stevens among others. While we couldn't be sure how things would pan out, we knew we had enough ability to make a fist of it.

We also had Ricky Hill on the right wing, who I always thought was a supremely gifted player. He supplied a lot of our goals and the only thing that I found mystifying about his career was that he never had the chance to play for a bigger club. He was more than good enough.

Maybe we were a couple of experienced players away from being a really good side because, despite all the talent we had, we were still dropping too many points.

A run of six defeats in eight games between February and April left us second bottom and hanging on grimly, just one place off the foot of the table. But back-to-back home wins over Aston Villa and Birmingham City gave us a chance of staying up and we looked as though we might just limp over the line.

Playing for the England Under-21s proved something of a welcome distraction at the time. I had started my first full match against Greece at the Karaiskaki Stadium in Piraeus the previous November, losing 2-1. The second leg was in March and we won 1-0 at Fratton Park – a ground which again had played a prominent role in my progress having made my reserve team debut for Charlton there as well – to go through to the next round on away goals.

I scored the only goal against Hungary at Newcastle United's St James' Park a month later to move into the last eight of Under-21s Championship.

But there was a bigger issue looming in my mind. Though I'd scored 15 goals and had a good, solid season, there was a chance it would all count for nothing as we went into our last game third from bottom and away to Manchester City.

City were just above us in the table and knew a point would be enough to guarantee their survival, whereas we needed to win to stay up and send City down – that was the only result that would save us from relegation.

We stayed in a hotel well outside Manchester near Stoke-on-Trent and heard that City were expecting a crowd of more than 43,000 as the magnitude of the game began to gradually sink in. The nerves were kicking in as we left the hotel and though we knew we were the underdogs, it was effectively a one-off game and anything was possible.

We'd already beaten City 3-1 at Kenilworth Road earlier in the season so we knew we were capable of coming away with the result we needed. But the importance of the occasion was almost too much for both teams, with the nerves and tension almost unbearable. I was fairly anonymous in all honesty and as each minute passed, we edged a little closer to the trapdoor. We knew we'd have to go for it at some stage, even if it meant conceding a goal – it didn't matter either way because a draw was no good to us.

The crowd were on pins and I remember City's Nicky Reid leaning into me at one point and saying, 'You're going down you little cunt!' I had no comeback because I was thinking, 'Yeah, you're right. We are.'

Then, with about 15 minutes remaining, Raddy Antic came on as a sub to give us more options in attack as Pleat had one last throw of the dice. I always remember Raddy, he was a really talented player who loved to nutmeg people, but I'm not sure Pleaty trusted him entirely. I think he thought that he'd use skill over safety nine times out of ten and this hadn't been the right situation for him to start. That said, he was the type of player who might just nick us a goal.

The crowd had bitten their fingernails down to the bone and desperate tackles were flying in as the clock ticked on towards full time. City had done pretty much everything but score but it just wouldn't go in for them as our goal lived something of a charmed life.

It was still 0-0 as we went into the final few minutes and launched what was a rare attack. You could sense the tension and anxiety among the City fans as we poured forward, knowing we had to find a goal from somewhere. I remember Graham Baker winning a challenge for City in midfield with a crunching challenge, but the ball ran loose and we won possession back.

A pass went out to Brian Stein on the right and his first cross was cleared by Tommy Caton, my old England Youth team-mate, but only back to Stein who whipped in another cross, higher this time.

City's keeper Alex Williams threw himself at the ball and punched it to the edge of the box, where Raddy was waiting. He hit a first-time volley back past Williams and several defenders to score what would be the only goal of the game.

The whole dynamic of the game had changed now we'd gone into the lead – suddenly we were staying up and City were facing relegation. The minutes that remained seemed to take an eternity and are a complete blur but at last the final whistle went and against all the odds, we'd done it. I decided not to say anything to Nicky Reid – well, not immediately!

Next thing I saw Pleaty skipping across the pitch celebrating, but that's when things got a bit hairy because thousands of angry City fans came onto the pitch as well.

A few of our lads were punched or involved in scuffles until police on horseback managed to pave a way through for us to make it to the relative safety of the tunnel. That's where I mullered Nicky Reid with an abusive rant that left him in no doubt that I was pleased that we'd be staying up and he'd be going in the other direction.

Even the crowd trouble couldn't take the gloss off the win and we celebrated with a few beers in the dressing room. We then showered, got changed and had a few more drinks in the players' bar before boarding the coach to leave the ground.

We were told to crouch down low and the curtains were pulled across because we expected the windows to come in, but the police escorted us clear of the ground and the driver put his foot down until we were out of Manchester. We reached our hotel in Stoke, broke out the Champagne and all got ridiculously pissed.

MISSION IMPOSSIBLE

It was a fantastic night and all the more enjoyable because nobody expected us to survive.

In hindsight, I think it was an easier game for us to approach because we knew what we had to do whereas City must have been in two minds – what do you do? Play it cagey? Go out for a goal so we had to score two?

It's an amazing memory and for me, it was more exciting than winning the FA Cup final, which I did a few years later. Against all the odds, little Luton Town had lived to fight another day.

06

Little England

Having survived relegation and had a decent first season on the top flight, I was included in the full England squad for the 1983 Home Internationals away to Northern Ireland and at home to Scotland, though I didn't actually play in either match. It was great to train with some of the best players in the country and it all augured well for the future, but I still had learn the protocol expected from top-level footballers.

After the game against Scotland, manager Bobby Robson gave us all a few days off and told us to meet up again at High Wycombe to continue the training camp where the squad for an upcoming tour of Australia would be announced.

When we got back at the hotel after the game, there was a party in full swing and nobody seemed to object when a few of us wandered into the bar area to grab a quick drink. A little while later and Paul Mariner and Terry Butcher were performing their best moves on the dance floor and everyone was having a good laugh – nothing too rowdy or over the top – until Don Howe, Bobby Robson's No.2, suddenly appeared with a face like thunder.

He was pissed off that we were drinking and fooling around in such a public location. He ordered everyone out and because I was there as well, I think he was a bit disappointed with me. The next time I saw Bobby Robson he just said, 'Just don't piss it all up the wall, Paul.'

Robson was short and concise and got his point across. I felt he was just giving me a bit of fatherly advice rather than a telling off, because he'd been in the game long enough to see careers go off the rails before they'd even really begun. I got the feeling he'd said that because he liked me and that I was in his plans going forward.

A few days later, I learned I'd been selected for the two-week tour of Australia, where I would see my first real action with the national team. The tour would include three games against the Aussies, with the first match in Sydney, the second in Brisbane before we finished the tour in Melbourne.

I made my debut in the first game at Sydney Cricket Ground. Because it wasn't designed for football to be played there, the pitch was odd, uneven with sloping sides where the ground ran away to the boundary. There were 28,000 people in a ground that had an 80,000-capacity, so it was a bit of a flat atmosphere and, in all honesty, a little surreal.

I came on as a sub and I remember chasing the ball along the wing before it just ran away from me and down the slope as I went to cross it into the box. We drew 0-0 and Robson said to me later, 'You need to be better in situations like that.'

I don't think he'd factored in that we were playing on a cricket field but apart from that, I never had any lengthy conversations with him, which I regret because he was a good manager and knowledgeable guy.

I hung around with a group that included Sammy Lee, Derek Statham, Gordon Cowans and Gary Shaw. We were known as 'The Big Five' – I'm not exactly sure why. We became pretty tight, mainly because we felt a bit on the outside. None of us were really established with England and we all felt comfortable in each other's company.

The older pros tended to stick together and that's just the way it was. I scored what would prove to be my only England goal in the second match of the tour where I also played from the start, making my full debut.

I played upfront alongside Trevor Francis who was a player I really admired. I was keen to learn as much as I could on the tour playing with some of the best players in Europe.

The goal I scored was nothing special but it proved to be the winner as we edged the game against Australia 1-0 – it was no more than just a toe-poke into the net from close range, but it was still a proud moment and I was happy that I'd got off the mark. I played in the final game of the tour as we drew 1-1, but I'd enjoyed the experience of being away and had done well.

I had no reason to think I didn't have a lengthy international future ahead of me, so long as I kept doing what I had been doing at club level.

Unfortunately, my England career was set to be short-lived and, back home, my second season with Luton would also be my last. I was enjoying my time at Kenilworth Road but I had aspirations to play for a bigger club and had been disappointed when none of teams I'd been linked with in the papers actually came in for me at Charlton.

Playing under David Pleat had allowed me to have the sort of freedom that brought the very best out of me, but the fact was I'd never win a title or play in Europe with Luton – the facilities at Kenilworth Road were a daily reminder of the limitations the club faced.

The camaraderie among the lads was really good and we were still on a bit of a high after surviving relegation at City. We initially took that feelgood factor into the our second season in Division One. We'd strengthened the squad too and I think I played a part – I'm not sure how big – in Luton going back to Charlton to sign another promising talent in Paul Elliott.

I remember Pleaty asking me what I thought of Elliott as a player and I just said that I found him difficult to play against and that he was strong, quick and was a great lad off the pitch as well. I'd been friends with Paul and knew his two brothers for a long time. We'd all grown up in the same neighbourhood, with the Elliott family living at the top of my road.

Whether my testimony was enough to make his mind up or not, I'm not sure, but Elliott signed not too long after and was a great addition to the squad. He was a couple of years younger than me and had always been quick.

One of my earliest memories of him at Charlton was when we were kids. We were playing forwards versus defenders and I took the ball past him and thought left him in my wake, only for him to come back and win the ball with a fantastic tackle. The truth was I'd never had an easy game against Paul and there weren't that many defenders I couldn't get the better of one way or another. I was happy he was now on board.

Though a fair bit had happened in a short space of time, I was still on a learning curve and appreciated the fact that Pleat kept things fairly simple when we played. We operated a straight 4-4-2 with no special routines for corners or free-kicks.

I had no particular defensive duties assigned to me – I was just expected to be ready when the ball came to me so we could try and do some damage going forward.

Pleat had us well drilled, everyone knew their job and got on with it. I loved the skipper Brian Horton to bits, but on the pitch he was the biggest moaner I've ever come across. His favourite line was 'give it easy!', so when I beat three players and stuck the ball past the keeper in one game, Brian was jumping on my back celebrating and I just turned to him and said, 'Why the fuck didn't I just give it easy?'

We played good, attacking football with Stein, Hill and Moss always a handful for any side. Because of our attacking style and willingness to entertain, I believe we deserved another crack at the top flight. I think teams thought they could bully us because we had a lot of flair players in the team, but we could handle ourselves and gave as good as we got.

The challenges back then were meatier and it was accepted that you might get hurt every now and then, but it wasn't a big deal. If someone left their foot in on you, you made sure you did the same back when the opportunity came along.

We started the 1983/84 season well and won three of our first six games to move up to seventh. I celebrated my 21st birthday with a 1-0 home win over Aston Villa and then a fancy dress party at the club in the evening. Then quite a few of us moved on to a nightclub in town. I had an American football uniform on and the other lads were dressed up as various characters, superheroes or whatever, with everyone getting into the spirit of it.

My girlfriend Melissa was there along with Wayne Turner and his future wife Nicki. A few of the lads were having a great laugh and enjoying ourselves with Wayne dressed in the full Freddie Starr Nazi outfit – he wore a German helmet, grey suit, swastika, shorts and wellies – the lot.

It was comical because he was getting shit from someone in a bar, which was par for the course for him, and he'd ended up smashing this guy over the head with his helmet. You couldn't have made it up; it was so ridiculous and it brought the evening to a premature end.

I felt sorry for him because it seemed like there was always a problem with someone who wanted to have a go at him. I'd had the same sort of thing at Charlton, so I knew what it was like to be a local lad made good – it just rattles some people's cages, whether through jealousy or whatever.

It wasn't healthy for Wayne and it did make me wonder whether moving away from Luton might be the only answer, as I couldn't see the small-town mentality of some of the locals changing any time soon.

For me though, things were fine. I continued to thrive under Pleaty, who let me play my game, always picked me and never tried to change me as a player. The other lads would no doubt say the same thing.

We went into our game at the end of October against Liverpool in fourth spot, three points behind leaders Manchester United and one behind Liverpool, with a better goal difference than all of them. After our exploits at Anfield the year before I was really looking forward to playing there again, but this time they were better prepared for us. We were taught something of a lesson as they thrashed us 6-0.

The funny thing is, I probably played better than I had during the 3-3 draw a year before! I nutmegged Alan Kennedy on the left, chipped Bruce Grobbelaar and hit the bar and had a really good all-round game, but ended with nothing to show for my efforts.

As we came off at the final whistle, Ian Rush walked over to me, shook my hand and said, 'I can't believe I've just scored five goals and you were man-of-the-match.' It was nice to hear that from a striker of his calibre.

I was enjoying my football and was feeling more confident than ever. The bigger the stage, the better I played, with that old show-off side of my nature I'd had since I was a kid coming the fore again.

I was being linked with a number of top clubs again, with Spurs, Manchester United and Liverpool all rumoured to be monitoring me. I never let the speculation distract me on the pitch and I continued to find the back of the net regularly.

Six weeks after the Anfield thrashing I timed a hat-trick away to Stoke City to perfection, as I discovered afterwards that former Liverpool boss Bob Paisley had been sat in the stands watching me. Fate played a part because I almost didn't play that day – I'd been nursing a heavy cold and had been moaning all morning about how rough I felt.

So much so that in the dressing room before the game the lads presented me with a huge dummy because apparently I'd been crying like a baby about the my man flu. I had to smile!

I was given a nip of brandy, as we did back then, and then went out and scored three goals, so maybe I had been making a mountain out of a molehill.

In fact, that mauling at Anfield hadn't destroyed our confidence as many predicted it would. Wins over West Brom and Notts County in the next two games put us into third spot on Boxing Day, which was incredible for a club our size and with the resources we had.

We were five points behind leaders Liverpool and just two behind second-placed Manchester United, so we really were mixing it with the big boys. Averaging almost two goals per game, we were there on merit, too.

I doubt anyone saw us as genuine title contenders but it gave our fans a chance to dream for a while. Unfortunately, that's as good as got our season imploded thereafter. At least the points we had in the bag would save us from the drop as we embarked on a run that was even worse than the one we'd suffered after Christmas the previous season.

We would win just three of our next 24 league and cup games – including a galling 4-3 FA Cup loss to bitter rivals Watford under the lights at Vicarage Road – a great game in which I scored twice but Mo Johnston scored the winner in extra- time.

Out of the cup and sliding down the table, we steadily went from title challengers to relegation candidates over the course of a few months.

We were something of a Jekyll and Hyde team and it's a bit of mystery why we played so well in the first half of the season and so poorly in the second for successive campaigns.

My theory was that the passing style we played meant we weren't as effective on the muddy pitches that were par for the course from January and February onwards. I think that played a big part in the downturn in our fortunes. The poor run didn't stop me being selected for England again though, as I was part of the team that lost 2-0 to France in February 1983.

I was up front with Brian Stein, who won what would be his only full cap that night. France had players like European Footballer of the Year Michel Platini, Joel Bats, Jean Tigana, Alain Giresse, Patrick Battiston and Maxime Bossis in their team – they were one of the best sides in the world at that time so there was no disgrace in losing to them.

We had Glenn Hoddle, Bryan Robson, Terry Butcher and Peter Shilton among our starting XI and it was the strongest England side I'd played in, but Platini was different class and scored two second half goals at the Parc des Princes in Paris. Whatever the result, it was good to know I was still in Bobby Robson's plans going forward.

The senior call-up meant I missed England Under-21s' European Championship quarter-final first leg win over France but the lads won 6-1 in my absence. I was back for the second leg, which was no more than a formality, as I continued to flit between the senior and Under-21 squads. In a way, that would work against me as time went on.

My overall efforts that season at club level meant that in mid-April I was informed I'd been voted the PFA Young Player of the Year. To be voted as the best by your fellow professionals meant a lot to me and it was ever sweeter considering I'd been up against Watford's Nigel Callaghan and John Barnes, who I thought had both had really strong seasons, as well as Ian Rush who had won it the year before.

I was a bit nervous picking up the trophy in London at the

PFA annual awards ceremony, where I had to give a speech in front of about a thousand people. Wayne was along with me and at events like that, you're always wandering around talking to people, having a few beers or whatever.

As a result, I had a few too many. As some mates and I headed off to celebrate, I left the award under the table we'd been sitting at! I returned an hour or so later to find it was still under the table.

I missed the England Under-21 semi-final matches against Italy through injury, but the lads won 3-1 win at Maine Road with future Manchester City boss Roberto Mancini ironically playing for the Italians.

We won the return 1-0 in Florence to progress to the final and as long as I was fit, I felt I was sure to play. However, that's when things came to an abrupt end thanks to series of fortunate – and unfortunate – events.

I didn't know it at the time but my last game for England was a 1-0 defeat to Wales at The Racecourse Ground in Wrexham in May 1984. I played alongside Tony Woodcock, with Mark Hughes scoring the only goal on 17 minutes. I thought there would be plenty of better days in an England shirt, but that would be the end of my international career at all levels.

07

Seeing Red

David Pleat made me laugh. He had his ways and was a real character. Some of these characteristics showed when Liverpool, who had been heavily linked with me in the papers for a number of months, finally made their move a couple of weeks before the end of the season.

He phoned me to say the deal was done, the fee had been agreed subject me being happy with the terms and that Liverpool wanted to meet me. I was massively excited by the prospect because one moment I'd been drifting towards the end of a disappointing season with Luton, the next I was about to join the most successful club in English football.

Pleaty said we needed to go to a hotel near Heathrow to talk with Liverpool chairman John Smith and chief executive Peter

Robinson and that he'd pick me up and take me there himself. He arrived not long after in his big Opel Senator. I jumped in and we exchanged small talk and set off. When we were maybe 15 minutes from Heathrow, he pulled over and said he was just nipping in to get a paper, asking, 'Do you want to drive the rest of the way, Paul?' I shrugged and said, 'Yeah, fine, if you want.'

I was wondering what the hell he was up to and didn't quite suss it out at the time. Looking back, I think he was just trying to see how nervous I was about the transfer.

The truth was, I wasn't bothered at all at that point and I was quite happy to drive his big three-litre car. But by the time we arrived at the hotel and the meeting was looming, I was suddenly a bag of nerves as the reality of the situation began to sink in.

Sheepishly I met Smith and Robinson from Liverpool and we all sat down to discuss the move. The talks went well and when they told me what the financial package was going to be – loads more than I was on at Luton – the final hurdle had been cleared. Money was never going to be an issue really because I was never going to turn down the chance to play for a club like Liverpool.

I was on cloud nine and felt all the hard work and self-belief had finally paid off. I'd enjoyed my time at Luton, I'd developed as a player under David Pleat but I was never going to win cups or titles with them. I owed a lot to the club and to Pleaty for believing in me and giving me the stage I had needed to perform on in the top flight. I'd done really well against Liverpool on successive visits to Anfield, which must have helped make up their minds to buy me.

I still had to complete the season with Luton though, and the events of the final few weeks actually made leaving a lot easier. Though Brian Stein and I weren't the best of mates, we weren't the worst of enemies, either. I never felt any real warmth from Steiny but he could be a decent lad when he wanted to be and he was someone I felt could have won more England caps than the one he actually did.

I think he could have probably played for a bigger club, too, had he had the breaks at the right time. I don't know why we never really hit it off but the root of the problem – I think – was that there was an element of resentment from the word go. Maybe it was because I hadn't contributed to Luton's promotion.

He'd been at Luton for five years when I joined and his goals meant he was the main man at the club for most of that time. His partnership with Steve White had been a major factor in Luton's rise. With White going to Charlton, maybe he felt sorry for his old partner and perhaps wasn't convinced I was the man to replace him – I couldn't say for sure.

I'll probably never know the reason but, if it was because of that, I don't think there was much I could have done about it.

Steiny had been flying during the first season I was at the club until he broke his foot around Christmas and was ruled out for five months, just when he had been approaching his peak.

Our form had dipped dramatically while he recovered so everyone knew he was integral to the team. Sometimes you get the breaks you want; sometimes you get the ones you don't.

The bottom line was I enjoyed playing alongside him and we had a good understanding, which developed into an effective partnership. The fact is you just get on with some team-mates better than others, just as you do with people in all walks of life.

WALSHY

We were never going to be close but I thought we'd managed to get through my time with Luton without any major fall-outs when suddenly all hell broke loose. We were away to West Ham in April 1984 when Steiny really spat his dummy out.

The team had been on a terrible run and everything we tried seemed to go wrong, with morale low and tempers frayed. There was one point towards the end of the game when I saw an opportunity and took a shot, but obviously Steiny felt he'd been better placed to score.

'Just pass the ball you cunt!' he said as we walked back towards the halfway line. I wasn't having that and I doubt you'll be surprised to hear that I gave as good as I got in return. The verbals flew back and forth for a few minutes before the ref called time on a 3-1 defeat.

We were both pumped up as we went back into the dressing room. I was pouring a cup of tea when a boot hit me on the back of the head. Stein had thrown it at me, so I was over to him in a flash. The fists were flying for a few seconds before we were separated, with the other lads holding us both back.

I was shouting, 'I'm not playing with that cunt again! You can fuck off' and he was shouting back, 'Fuck off! I'm not playing with that cunt again!' There was some nasty stuff said by both of us and it was always going to be hard to rectify the situation after that.

Steiny and the other lads were aware I was going to move on because it had been all over the papers for a few weeks, so it wasn't a situation that was going to fester. However, Pleat now had a dilemma because although he knew I was leaving, Stein wasn't going anywhere.

So he couldn't really take sides and had to be straight down the middle, no matter what he really thought about it all. The two of us did play together again a couple of times but it was all about tolerating each other for a few more days rather than building any bridges.

A 3-0 away defeat to West Brom would be my last game for Luton Town. We'd survived the drop thanks to our early season form and I was glad I left the club as an established First Division side, plus they were getting decent money for me.

The time had come for me to travel to Merseyside and sign for Liverpool but there was nothing ordinary about the day itself, which turned out to be bizarre from start to finish.

I was getting ready to leave Madge at my digs when a distressed knock came at the back door. It was Rose from next door and she was in a state because her husband George had just collapsed. I went with her next door and there he was, lying on the floor. I didn't even know if he was still alive.

It turned out he had angina and had suffered a heart attack. He clearly wasn't in a good way. There was another neighbour there as well and if I'm honest, I didn't fancy giving him the kiss of life, but told her what to do.

I said, 'Take his teeth out, pinch his nose and then blow into his mouth a few times before pumping his heart.' She followed the instructions and as I watched her, however callous it might sound, I was relieved it wasn't me. It didn't look pleasant.

The paramedics arrived shortly after, but it was too late and he'd already gone – the medics said there was probably nothing we could have done for him anyway. I felt terrible because as much as I wanted to comfort Rose, I knew I had to get a move on and get to the station.

I was going to sign for Liverpool – something that didn't

happen every day. I was in a really awkward situation, with Rose distraught and her husband dead on the floor, while all I was thinking of was not missing my train! You couldn't have made a more awkward situation up.

I like to think of myself as a decent bloke and I've probably had better moments, but the fact was I had to go. I gave Rose a hug and said how sorry I was, then I was on my way. I left for the station wondering if all that had really just happened. Bizarre didn't even come close.

I still didn't have any representation at that point, but I'd recently met agent Eric Hall, who was more in the music business than football. He wanted to get his foot in the door and so helped organise one or two aspects of the deal.

He felt he wasn't experienced enough to actually represent me yet, so he asked his lawyer Brian Fuger to accompany me to Merseyside instead. We met up with Joe Fagan and John Smith to finalise the finer points of the deal.

We started talking numbers again and Liverpool had a figure in mind but didn't want to go much higher. Save for a few tweaks, we came to an agreement fairly quickly. I signed the contract and I was now officially a Liverpool player, but Fagan was just about to give me a problem.

He said, 'Paul, we want you to come to the European Cup final in Rome with us and then come along to Swaziland with the lads for an end-of-season tour and get to know everyone a bit better.'

I thought it sounded fantastic at the time and even better when he added, 'And there will be £1,000 for you to spend on the trip, too,' which was a fair wad at the time.

Liverpool paid almost £1m to take me to Anfield and I left the meeting feeling exhilarated. I called Pleaty from Lime Street station and told him the deal was sealed.

The problem I had was the final of the European Under-21 Championship against Spain was coming up. The first leg was in Seville in just a few days' time but I really wanted to travel with Liverpool to Rome and Africa.

I asked Pleaty whether he thought Bobby Robson would mind if I didn't travel with the Under-21s on this occasion, as I really wanted to bed in at Liverpool as quickly as I could.

My understanding of the situation was that I already had five full England caps and was sure to tour South America with the senior squad in the summer, so I felt confident that I was part of Robson's plans.

It was difficult because I felt pulled in several directions. I wanted to meet my new team-mates and, in truth, I also felt more of a full international than an Under-21 player anyway, with Robson withdrawing me from one game to play for the senior team shortly before. However, I wasn't seeing the bigger picture and that assumption was a major mistake.

The bottom line was I'd played about 60 games that season and I was completely fucked and needed to recharge my batteries before I burned myself out. In hindsight, that's how I should have approached the issue.

The thought of having a bit of a breather with Liverpool, seeing Rome and Africa and getting a grand for the privilege made complete sense to me at that time, because I could then go on the South American tour in three weeks refreshed and ready to go again.

The fact is, I should have been a bit harder on myself and gone with the Under-21s, sacrificed Rome and Swaziland and played for England instead. But I'd had my head turned and honestly didn't see it as a major problem at the time. So I asked Pleaty's advice and he said he would call Bobby Robson on my behalf and see what he had to say.

The thing is, I'm not quite sure how Pleaty portrayed me during that telephone conversation. Did he say bluntly, 'Bobby, Paul can't travel to the Under-21s final as he's going away with Liverpool instead'? Or did he say, 'Maybe the lad needs a break?'

The truth is I'm not sure what was said and the bottom line is I should have called Bobby Robson myself and explained the situation and how I saw things. If he'd even hinted that it was in my best interests to play for the Under-21s, I would have done so without hesitation. All know is that I never played for England again.

I didn't have to wait long to find out what his reaction was, either. The next day, I went to buy a paper and the headline on the back was 'Bobby boots out Walsh!' with Robson saying, 'If he can't motivate himself to play in a European Under-21 final, he's not for me.'

But instead of calling Bobby up to try to sort things out and maybe better explain the situation, I just left it. I thought I'd get back in the England team sooner or later when things calmed down a bit, which was more naivety on my part.

I thought that playing for a team like Liverpool, surely it would only be a matter of time before I played my way back into his plans. But Robson had other ideas and, at that point, I wasn't about to backtrack either.

It was quite interesting because my England Under-21 strike partner Mark Hateley was playing for Portsmouth in Division

Two. I'd just signed for Liverpool, had won the PFA Young Player award and enjoyed a great season, yet it was Hateley who replaced me on the tour of South America.

Of course, on that trip he scored a back-post header against Brazil the night John Barnes also bagged his wonder goal. England secured a first win in 45 years over Brazil as well as a first ever victory on Brazilian soil. It launched the careers of Barnes and Hateley into a different stratosphere, with Hateley swapping Pompey for AC Milan in a million-quid deal shortly afterwards. I still can't help wonder 'what if?'

Hateley became England's centre-forward for the next few years and then Gary Lineker and Peter Beardsley came on the international scene, making competition even tougher.

So as long as Robson was in charge, there would be no place for me. The fact was he had some more than decent alternatives that were working well for him and the bottom line was I don't think he ever forgave me. Putting it plain and simple, I made the wrong decision and paid for it. It's still the biggest regret of my career.

Brotherly love: Aged 18 months with brother Mark

On the ball: Me and my brother Mark in the back garden at Abbeywood with our dog Sally – Mark's wearing the West Ham shirt

Bad hair day: The first signs of a dodgy Barnet, aged 11 or so

Class pals: On a campsite in Gosfield with my school mates, 1976

Rising talent: At The Valley, posing for the local paper after playing for England Youth (right) and with my mum and dad (below)

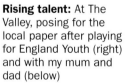

Soap star: caught in the shower at the age of 18 while at Charlton

Match ball: my first hat-trick ball for the goals I scored against Brentford for Charlton

Honoured: Clutching the Young Player of the Month award for October 1981

Hatters hero: In full Luton Town kit – the club I played for from 1982-84

Card happy: Reading a Valentine's card on the team bus in 1983

Man in the mirror: Keeping the hair in good condition in October 1983

Signing in: Shaking hands with Luton Town manager David Pleat in July 1982

Walshy winner: This shot beat Nevill Southall and clinched a 1-0 win for Luton against Everton at Goodison Park in October 1983

England calling: In action against Luxembourg in 1982 (left) and before a win against Hungary

ernational class: I was part of the England set-up with Bryan Robson, aham Rix, manager Bobby Robson and Kenny Sansom in January 1984

Head-hunted: With David Hodgson and Alan Kennedy after
Liverpool's European Cup win at a hilltop villa in Rome

Instant impact: It took me only one minute to score on my first appearance as a Liverpool player at Anfield in a 3-0 win against West Ham in August 1984

Double disappointment: My first season at Liverpool in 1984/85 started with a substitute appearance in a 1-0 Charity Shield defeat to Everton and ended with a 1-0 European Cup final loss to Juventus at Heysel Stadium – not that the result mattered

Sing when you're winning: In the studio (back row, third from the left) recording Liverpool's FA Cup final song in 1986 with the rest of the squad

Wat a season: Two goals against Watford in January 1986 helped Liverpool to a 3-2 win as the club went on to seal a league and cup double at Wembley

Goal rush: The second goal of a hat-trick against Norwich in November 1986

Kop that: Celebrating at Anfield after a goal in a 2-0 win against Newcastle in January 1987

08

When in Rome...

I wasn't unduly concerned about the future with England as I flew out to Rome ahead of the European Cup final, because I believed the situation would resolve itself. England Under-21s had won both legs to be crowned champions of Europe, so my absence hadn't unduly affected the team. I hoped that would help, too.

I was relaxed and happy when I joined my new team-mates for the first time as they went out for a training session in preparation for playing Roma. To my mind, there was no question I'd made the right decision to travel to Italy and what had happened was all in the past.

There were no airs and graces about the Liverpool lads at all – they weren't Big Time Charlies, even if they have had every right to be. There were holes in the training kit, everything was pretty basic and they were happy to play football wherever they were asked to.

On the morning of the final we all trained on a gravel pitch near the hotel, which was no more than Sunday League standard. It was quite refreshing considering they were about to play the biggest club game in the world.

I was a bit nervous because it was my first knock-around with them all and I had no idea what they thought about me.

I remember looking around and seeing Graeme Souness, Kenny Dalglish, Mark Lawrenson, Alan Hansen, Ronnie Whelan, Ian Rush, Sammy Lee, Bruce Grobbelaar, Alan Kennedy, Phil Neal – plus many others – and thinking it was unbelievable that I was now part of it all. They also had the small matter of a European Cup final in a few hours' time.

One of my main memories I had from that day was something I thought was a bit harsh on Phil Thompson. I didn't know what the protocol was as we left the hotel for the Olympic Stadium so I went to board the first coach. Manager Joe Fagan told me I was to travel on the bus behind, which had wives and journalists on, and that was fine by me.

I was new and I wasn't part of the team that had made it to the final so I had no problem being told that, but behind me was Thommo. I heard Fagan say, 'No, no, Phil. You need to get on the second bus, too.' I turned around and could see he was devastated. He was a diehard Liverpool fan who had won everything with the club and made close to 500 appearances yet it counted for nothing at that moment.

I felt for him but it taught me that there was a another side to the club that seemed to suggest that if you weren't in, you were out. There wouldn't be any middle ground or sentiment. Maybe that harsh edge is what made them dominant for such a long time.

Former Liverpool striker David Johnson had left the club not long before the final but had travelled to Rome as a supporter. He didn't have a hotel room booked so he bunked in with me and Thommo at the team hotel the night before the game.

There was a single and a double bed and he took the single, meaning I had to share the double with Thommo. I woke up in the night to find there was something long and hard sticking in my back – but luckily it was only Thommo's nose!

At the Olympic Stadium, I made my way to the stands before kick-off with Dave Johnson and Thommo, who were both in good spirits and looking forward to the match. At the end of the day, they were massive Liverpool fans – but I wasn't and felt a bit out of it – so I decided to sit in between them instead and felt a bit more involved.

The game itself was tense but Liverpool beat Roma on penalties when Alan Kennedy smacked the winner after Bruce had done his famous 'spaghetti legs' routine. It was probably then it began to sink in that I was now playing for the champions of Europe. I'd come a long way in the space of a few years.

There was a party that night at a hilltop villa in Rome where a reception was held. Later we went back to the Holiday Inn hotel in the city where there were loads of Liverpool fans staying. As you might imagine, they were delirious, in high spirits and mostly pissed.

The lads just casually chatted and mixed with the supporters in the bar and the European Cup was passed around by everyone – it was ridiculous on some levels and fantastic in other ways. It was great to see how the players and fans had a genuine relationship. That was something I learned pretty quickly. Liverpool fans and the players had a real connection and that bond was a big part of the club's success over such a sustained period.

I should have taken the European Cup back to The Studio in Luton along with Wayne Turner and let those lads throw their beer at that instead of the big screens! It was a totally different mentality to what I'd experienced before, with much greater expectations to go with it.

We flew home the next day to Speke Airport and I was invited to join the open top bus tour around the city, which was an amazing, slightly surreal experience bearing in mind I'd only been part of it all for a couple of days.

There were tens of thousands on the streets to welcome the team home and though I enjoyed it, I felt a little sheepish because I'd played no part in the success the fans were celebrating. So I stayed in the background as much as possible and let the lads who'd done all the hard work enjoy themselves.

The whole day was a reminder of what a massive club I'd joined and I couldn't wait to really become part of celebrations like that on merit.

We stayed another day in Liverpool before flying out to Swaziland, which was nothing more than an excuse for a massive piss-up in reality – and why not? The lads deserved to let their hair down. We were staying at a hotel that was on a golf course and had a casino as well. It was absolutely rammed at the weekend with tourists and wealthy locals.

Tottenham were our opponents for the exhibition game we'd agreed to play. We were staying at the same complex as them but they were taking the game a bit more seriously than us. We were there to relax and enjoy ourselves while they were there to win.

On the day of the game, after a heavy night on the beer, the coaches went around the hotel trying to get a team together – well, anyone who was compos mentis and sober enough to play Spurs. It wasn't easy to round up a team and when they'd managed to get about 13 of us up, we headed off to the stadium all feeling worse for wear and wishing we were somewhere else.

Despite our state, we won 5-2. In fact, we battered Spurs who played quite well, but we just had too much for them – a measure of how good that team was.

Later that day, Graeme Souness, who was the equivalent of Killer at Charlton, appeared at the hotel bar. He hadn't played against Spurs and had probably rolled over and gone back to sleep when the coaches knocked on his room – let's face it, who was going to demand Graeme Souness played?

He came over to me smiling and put some money in my hand, saying, 'There you go, son.' I said thanks, then turned around and counted it – £500 – half the money I'd been promised. I wasn't best pleased – maybe Souness wondered why I was getting so much when I hadn't done anything yet for the club.

The fact was, I'd been told I was being paid a grand and it didn't matter what anyone else thought. I took a deep breath, went over to where he was standing and sheepishly tapped him on the shoulder. I said, 'I'm not being funny Graeme, but Peter Robinson told me I was getting a grand.'

He looked at me dead in the eye, half-sighed before he put his hand in his pocket, counted out £500 and almost threw it at me before walking off. He was quite an intimidating bloke and a great player, but I had to do what I thought was right. I didn't know whether that would cause any issues between me and him going forward, but I didn't really have time to find out. I didn't know it at the time, but he wasn't going to be around for much longer.

The next day we had a free day and a choice of what we wanted to do. We could go to Johannesburg, Sun City or Durban, so about ten of us decided to go to Durban in two little five-seater planes. We would be staying at a hotel right on the sea. It was fantastic and a different world to the one I'd been used to at Charlton and to a lesser extent Luton, where I had travelled around but not extensively.

Souness travelled with our party as well. We had a chat and a few drinks and he seemed like a good guy – but on the second day of the Durban trip, we were all by the pool enjoying a few cold beers in the sun when the concierge came over and said, 'Mr Souness, you've got a phone call.'

He nodded as though he was expecting it, went into the foyer and that was it. He packed his bags, left the hotel and caught a flight to Italy to sign for Sampdoria, never to be seen again. That's how quickly it happened.

I enjoyed the rest of the summer with Melissa and was excited at the prospect of my first season with Liverpool. I didn't have anywhere to live yet and I'd had it written into my contract that I would be staying at a hotel while I settled in to my new surroundings and found a house.

It turned out that John Wark and Kevin MacDonald were also staying there and, after a short trial just before the season started, Jan Molby also joined us. We all got on well and because we were right in the middle of the city centre and everything was accessible, we soon got to know each other. We often went out for a drink, meal or whatever to escape the boredom of our hotel rooms. Staying where we were, it meant we integrated ourselves into the city and understood what Liverpool was all about really quickly.

I found the training at Liverpool a bit different to what I'd expected. I'd imagined it would be hard, precision drilled routines and suchlike but I couldn't have been more wrong. We had two sticks and two bollards for goals across half of a pitch and that was as technical as it got.

Bruce Grobbelaar would play out as we had fly keepers and we'd play a 45-minute five-a-side session with either two-touch or all in. If the tempo was good, we wouldn't do any extra running and instead play another 45-minute game.

Bruce never did any keeper training and we didn't have any goalkeeper coaches, which I thought was a bit odd. But when you look at how many trophies the club won, it's hard to argue with their methods, even if they were somewhat unorthodox.

When you take into account all the quirky methods the club employed (and there were plenty more that I'd discover over the next few years), I find it amazing that they were so successful – but then maybe that was the secret of their success.

I soon discovered Joe Fagan didn't say that much while Ronnie Moran and Roy Evans put on a decent good cop/bad cop routine, where one would bawl you out while the other was more measured and supportive.

They all worked well together as a team, as many Boot Room members had done before them no doubt, and it was the 'Liverpool Way'. I just needed to get my head down in training, work hard in pre-season and see where I stood in the mix when the dust settled. We went to Switzerland on tour to build up everyone's match fitness and had a few friendlies, including one against Young Boys of Bern.

It was in Switzerland that I quickly realised the medical side of the club wasn't that great. In fact, it was bordering on amateurish. We didn't have a physio and Roy Evans only ran on with the magic sponge because he was younger, slimmer and faster than Ronnie Moran – Ronnie gave the treatment out in the dressing room because Roy ran on the pitch – and that's as scientific as it got.

I don't think Ronnie even had the basic qualifications for the job, which I thought was incredible for a club of Liverpool's size.

Luton's physio John Sheridan had been top drawer throughout my time at Kenilworth Road and eventually moved on to Spurs while Charlton Athletic had two qualified physios!

Liverpool had a club doctor who was getting on a bit and I remember having a back spasm before the game against Young Boys. He examined my back, had a prod and said, 'Is that where it's hurting?' I said it was and thought maybe I'd underestimated the club's methods after all. Then he went into his bag and gave me two aspirin!

That was it – no massage or further investigation. I wondered what difference that would make and started the game in some discomfort. Eventually I had to come off because I was in so much pain.

It wasn't how I wanted to start life at the club but the message was clear – they didn't want soft-arses or fannies – you played with knocks and you got on with it. But that way of thinking was already becoming a thing of the past, even in 1984.

WHEN IN ROME...

There's a fine line between being resilient and being asked to risk serious injury, but I put it down as a one-off and didn't think too much more about it. I should have known better with Ronnie and Reggie in charge of our welfare.

There was one comical moment with the club doctor that would have been more at home in a Carry On film. The doc lived in a house near Anfield and outside his front window there was a bus stop that had three or four people waiting at it when I arrived.

I'd gone to see him because I had a problem with piles. I knocked on the door and he answered and invited me in. It was dark and dingy inside and he showed me into his front room, where he switched the light on. But there was just a single stem bulb hanging down and it hardly made a difference.

He asked me to pull my trousers down but I knew it was too dark to see properly, so he asked me to move closer to the window so he could get a bit more light.

As I shuffled over, he opened the net curtains to get even more light in. As I bent over again, he said, 'Oh yes, I can see what the problem is.'

As I turned around to pull up my trousers, I could see everyone at the bus stop staring in at my arse! It was comical but thank-fully, by the time I came out of the house, the bus had collected the unwanted observers and I was saved the further embarrass-ment of them putting a face to the arse.

I remember arriving at Anfield a few days before the start of the season and having the team photo in front of the Kop, which felt eerie as an empty terrace.

I was looking forward to playing in front of the Liverpool fans and having that swaying mass behind me belting out You'll

WALSHY

Never Walk Alone. The thought sent shivers down my spine. I glanced around at my team-mates and took my place on the front row, where we had the Division One trophy, the European Cup and the League Cup lined up on the pitch.

I had to pinch myself that it was all really happening. I just had to find my place in the grand scheme of things so I could really start to feel at home.

09

The Darkest Night

I knew it was unlikely I would start the 1984/85 season as a first-choice striker because Ian Rush and Kenny Dalglish were going to be ahead of me to begin with. I accepted that, even though I fully intended to force my way in eventually.

I played plenty of times in pre-season and made my debut from the bench in the FA Charity Shield match against Everton in front of 100,000 Merseysiders at Wembley Stadium. I came on after 53 minutes, replacing David Hodgson. We ended up losing 1-0 after Alan Hansen cleared a ball off the line, straight into Bruce Grobbelaar's shins and back into the net just five minutes after I'd come on.

I expected to play here and there with some appearances off the bench in the early weeks of the new season but as it was,

WALSHY

I was handed my chance much earlier than I'd envisaged. Just before the season started, Ian Rush tore his cartilage and was ruled out for the first six weeks, so I was in for the opening game against Norwich City at Carrow Road.

I played alongside Kenny and did okay, but we drew 3-3 with Mick Channon equalising in the last minute for Norwich. I was happy I'd made my debut so early in the season and it felt good to know I'd have a good run in the first team so long as I took my chance.

My mum and dad came up for my home debut and things couldn't have gone much better. We were playing Dad's team, West Ham, and I scored after just 14 seconds – probably the most exhilarating feeling I'd had in my career and a dream start in front of the Liverpool fans.

I made another for John Wark, who scored twice and we went on to win 3-1– it was probably the happiest my dad had ever been after a West Ham defeat.

Growing up, Dalglish had been someone I'd wanted to emulate so to be playing alongside him now was a privilege, but the problem I had was that I couldn't understand a fucking word he said! I know it's funny but I found it a bit uncomfortable if I'm honest because there's only so many times you can say, 'Eh? What?'

There were so many Scots in our dressing room that when they were together, they'd gradually get broader and broader until it was like they were talking a different language.

I tended to shy away from Kenny to avoid further embarrassment, plus there was a 10-year age gap so we didn't often mix socially. However, the communication problem was a minor factor in what would develop into a troubled relationship.

THE DARKEST NIGHT

The fans seemed to take to me well, despite me being a Cockney – I honestly don't think too many had played for Liverpool before I arrived. Of course, scoring on my debut helped, but it was exciting to walk out and see 20,000 supporters crammed together on the Kop. I couldn't think of anywhere else I'd rather be at that moment in my career.

As the season progressed, we had a few dodgy results. Everton looked like being our biggest rivals for the title, but overall I felt I'd settled in well.

The old saying 'swings and roundabouts' sprang to mind as I picked up a knee injury in October 1984, having got my initial break because of Rush's injury. It came when things seemed to be going really well for me, but I felt my knee lock in training and knew I'd tweaked something.

I'd torn my cartilage, but as I stood there rubbing my knee Joe Fagan said, 'Look at Walshy – he thinks he's Ian Rush.' Of course, that made me want to play on all the more and by turning out against Spurs a few days later, I made things worse.

My knee went again during the game and a minor tear became a big one. I had to be stretchered off, knowing that I'd be out for four-to-six weeks as a result.

I was pissed off because nobody had diagnosed the problem and I lost confidence in our physio department – if you could call it that – and their lack of medical knowledge almost immediately. There has to be something wrong when there is a culture of being afraid to report an injury for fear of being labelled a soft-arse. Maybe it was my fault for not pushing it, because I knew things weren't right.

However, I was reluctant to tell them I aggravated the injury getting my toe caught in the hotel bed sheets as I neared a return, but I did and received a bollocking as a result, though it was with a wry smile. I was out for another fortnight.

As it was I returned by Christmas and had scored four league goals. I'd missed so many games and a lot of the time I was coming off the bench now Rushy had recovered from injury, so was finding it difficult to get any momentum going.

I'd scored a few European Cup goals – including one against Lech Poznan and two against Austria Vienna – which should have been a hat-trick except that I missed a late penalty. Despite winning 4-1, in the dressing room afterwards, Joe Fagan ripped into Ian Rush for letting me take the penalty. He said Rushy had been meant to take it and not to let it happen again. I wonder what he'd have said if I'd have scored?

Off the pitch I was feeling settled and happy. By February, Melissa and I finally moved out of the hotel we'd been staying in for eight months. I was the last to leave, with the other lads all finding other places to live more quickly than we had.

The time was right to find somewhere of our own. I'd always wanted a big house and with a lot of the lads recommending the Wirral, we started looking for around that area. It wasn't long before we found a place in Neston that needed a few bits doing to it. It was perfect and came with a tennis court and an acre of land.

I felt I'd come a long way from the terraced house I grew up in and it was somewhere I could drive towards and think 'Yeah, that's mine.' I wasn't massively into DIY but I enjoyed having a project I could get on with in the background. So we put in an offer, it was accepted and we moved in shortly afterwards.

That first season at Anfield ticked along nicely but it proved to be one where we fell just short in almost everything we were

involved in. I'd still really enjoyed it and felt I'd done my share
– it felt really good to be challenging for major honours instead
of constantly fighting relegation.

Maybe the highlight of the year was when we played
Manchester United in the FA Cup semi-final at Goodison Park.
Trailing 2-1 with just a minute of extra-time to play, Dalglish
swung in a cross, Rush's header was saved by Gary Bailey but
the ball fell to me a few yards out. It was between me and Kevin
Moran but I reacted marginally faster and bundled the ball over
the line to make it 2-2.

It was in front of our fans packed into the Gwladys Street
end and they just went mental. I'd never experienced a better
atmosphere or such a rush when I scored a goal – the only
disappointment was losing the replay 2-1 at Maine Road four
days later.

One thing that had made me feel like an important part of
the Liverpool squad in my first season was the way the club had
managed my fitness and been happy for me to play, then rest,
then play again, then rest and so on.

I wasn't training much and it showed where I was in their
thinking. The fact they had been prepared to let me miss
training in order to be fit for the weekend games meant I'd
become integral to the team far sooner than I'd expected.

While we only finished second in the league behind Everton,
we had reached the European Cup final once again where we
would face Juventus at the Heysel Stadium in Belgium. Had
we won that game and things had gone as planned, the season
would have been remembered as a fantastic success, but what
should have been the biggest night of my life turned into a
tragedy that still haunts so many people to this day.

It began when we arrived at Heysel and I couldn't help wondering how this run-down, ageing stadium had won the right to host such a huge game – I'd seen better lower league grounds in England. There were thousands of fans from both clubs milling around and, despite the occasion, I couldn't help but feel disappointed with the choice of venue.

Juventus had half the Italian national team playing for them so we knew it was going to be a really difficult game, but there was something in the air that night – something felt wrong.

I remember when we went out to look at the pitch and behind one goal, there was terracing with what looked like a make-shift fence going down the middle to segregate both sets of fans. There was an uncomfortable atmosphere and a lack of any properly organised segregation – it seemed to be inviting trouble.

I didn't see exactly what happened later, but apparently the fence was pushed over and the fans charged at each other. In the ensuing chaos, a supporting wall collapsed and 39 people were killed, while dozens were seriously injured.

Our dressing room was close to the wall that fell and it was only as kick-off approached we began to hear rumours that some people might have been killed. Phil Neal had to go on to the pitch to plead for calm among our fans and a lot of what happened afterwards is just a blur.

It had literally been a disaster waiting to happen and though plenty of people were quick to point the blame at the supporters, the truth was the stadium wasn't fit for purpose and the security measures had been a joke.

The match shouldn't have been played out of respect for the people had lost their lives or been injured and it should have been re-staged somewhere else at a later date. However, that was never going to happen with TV companies and sponsors probably pressuring UEFA to press on no matter what.

Eventually, we came out when the decision to play the match had been made on the basis that abandoning it could cause further disturbances. We'll never know if that was true and maybe there wasn't an obvious solution.

We did as we were asked and kicked off in a subdued, surreal atmosphere. There was debris all around the running track surrounding the pitch. It just seemed bizarre that we were actually playing football considering what had gone on and was still happening a few feet away from the pitch.

What should have been the biggest game of my life had turned out to be a nightmare, with the football itself almost immaterial. As professionals we did what we were asked but I was destined not to complete the game anyway. An injury I'd been carrying for several weeks worsened when I stretched for a cross towards the end of the first half. After that, I could barely walk and came off at the break.

I didn't even bother coming out for the second half and stayed in the dressing room as Juventus went on to win 1-0.

I have nothing but sad, disappointing memories from that night in Brussels. If I'm honest, when the Champions League final comes around each year, I look at the organisation, facilities and fantastic stadiums the games are played in today and wonder how the fuck we ever ended up playing at Heysel.

So it was Belgium's turn to host the final – so what? If they didn't have the facilities, they should have built a proper stadium or else lose their slot until they did.

Afterwards, English clubs were banned from Europe for five

years as a result of the deaths, with UEFA pointing the blame at the Liverpool fans. No questions were asked as to how the venue was deemed fit for a showpiece European final. It was yet another cop-out on their part in my opinion, but there are no surprises there – this was UEFA after all.

We went back to the hotel and drank for a few hours, trying to get the images we'd seen out of our heads. The news that Joe Fagan had decided to retire soon filtered through and that was disappointing for all of us. The Heysel disaster should not have been the way his time with Liverpool ended.

He was a good man and also the manager who'd taken me to the club – and the lads loved him. Everything was so sombre; we just needed to escape normality for a while. The next day we flew home to Liverpool, where it was announced Kenny Dalglish was taking over as player/manager.

It was a surprise to say the least. Kenny's appointment also meant I was now in the unique and unenviable position of having my boss as my main rival for a starting spot.

Things would be different from now on. Even though I knew Kenny was coming towards the end of his playing days, the standing he had among the Liverpool supporters meant the decision to make him the boss was a popular one.

However, it was still something of a gamble because he had no experience in management whatsoever. Only time would tell if it had been a wise move.

When I'd signed, it had been my understanding that Kenny was going to be gradually phased out of the first team and I was being groomed to fill his boots – that's why the club had bought me in the first place. Kenny staying on changed that whole dynamic.

THE DARKEST NIGHT

I wasn't sure what it meant for me going forward, but I had enough belief and confidence in my own ability to think I still had a bright future at Anfield.

I knew I was up against a bona fide Liverpool legend and the only thing I had on Kenny was age. That meant I'd probably play fairly regularly as he didn't have the legs to play week in, week out. It was going to be an interesting season.

10

Double Whammy

We'd returned to Merseyside to find the club was in the middle of a massive inquest and, with the events in Belgium plus Fagan's departure still fresh, my head was spinning. I just wanted to get away from everything for a while so Melissa and I decided to head back down south for a few weeks.

We visited her folks and it was good to see Pat and Bill Berry again and just get away from football for a bit. Bill noticed straight away that I wasn't walking properly and was in some discomfort. He knew I'd been struggling for a while so he told me to lie down flat on the floor and raise my right leg, then do the same with my left leg while he made a quick assessment.

The pain was severe. He pushed his finger onto one particular area that was excruciating before nodding and telling me that my problem was a hernia. The Liverpool medical verdict had been that my abductor muscle might have detached and possibly needed an operation. Once the surgeon back in Liverpool spoke to Bill, who explained the diagnosis and that there was no point in delaying the inevitable, he was happy for him to carry out the procedure.

Kenny wasn't overly impressed that I'd organised an operation myself, but he accepted that it made sense to get the problem resolved as quickly as possible and gave the go-ahead.

It meant I'd miss pre-season and probably the first few games of the 1985/86 campaign but I was determined to become first-choice partner for Ian Rush and build on what had been a solid first season with the Reds. I went under the knife, rested for a few days and gradually started to build my strength up again.

I'm not sure why, but in late August there were rumours in the papers that Aston Villa were interested in signing me and the stories carried on for a week or so.

I decided to speak to Kenny and clarify the situation because although I'd played alongside him for a year, I still wasn't sure where I stood with him. At the end of the day, I wasn't a player he'd signed.

I went into his office and he looked up at me. 'What's all this about Aston Villa in the papers?' I asked and quick as a flash, he said, 'Why, do you want to go?' I said that I didn't and he said, 'Well don't worry about it then,' and carried on with whatever he'd been doing.

I'm not sure what he thought I was going to say to that, but it was a typical Dalglish clever-bollocks response. Maybe he'd wanted me to say yes so he could move me on – or maybe not – but I had no intention of leaving Anfield at that stage. I could never figure out what he was thinking and I never really got to the bottom of the rumours.

I continued to build up my fitness and by the end of the month I was fit enough to play for the reserves, though I was nowhere near being ready for first team. After a couple of goals against Newcastle United reserves a few weeks later I was recalled to the squad and named as sub for the trip to Oxford United.

With 20 minutes gone, Ronnie Whelan came off with a gashed forehead and I replaced him. By half-time, we were 2-0 down and playing poorly, with the whole team out of sorts and unable to get going.

I sat down and waited for Kenny to give us all a bit of a bollocking, but I seemed to be his only focus. He leaned into me and said, 'See you? You're not even trying.'

Now sometimes you play well and sometimes you don't, but one thing nobody had ever accused me of was not trying. It's just not in my DNA and no matter how low I was feeling, I'd never give less than everything I had.

I'd been pissed off at being left out of the team because I'd felt ready for a couple of weeks and, by that point, I'd had enough. I just snapped and said, 'You can fuck off, you Scottish cunt! Don't ever accuse me of not trying – now fuck off!'

Kenny paused for a moment and then said, 'There will only be one person fucking off, and that's you.' I just nodded. 'Yeah? Well fucking get on with it then.'

I asked to be put on the transfer list and I thought that would be that as far as my time at Liverpool was concerned. I thought the damage was irreparable and there would probably be no way back. Surprisingly though, it didn't turn out that way at all and eventually things settled down. A few weeks later I asked to be taken off the list and my second season at Anfield instead turned out to be my best in a red shirt.

I was dropped for a couple of weeks after the bust-up which I fully expected, but after a couple of goals against Everton in the reserves, I was back in the team. From there I went from strength to strength. I was feeling sharp and back to full fitness and I was started in the game against QPR, scoring our only goal in a 2-1 defeat.

The early season issues were soon forgotten and I hit a rich vein of form, which saw me bag 12 goals in 14 games. I couldn't have been happier as we powered our way towards the title.

I was scoring goals regularly, enjoying my football and felt settled both on and off the pitch – with my relationship Kenny better than it had been for a while.

I'd sold the house in Neston after less than a year and moved into the Moat House Hotel in Paradise Street, a place run by Jack Ferguson who was also a good friend of Kenny's.

Melissa and I told Jack I needed a place to stay for several weeks and that I had my boxer dog Clyde to look after, too. He told me he had a suite with two double bedrooms, two bathrooms and another room that we – including the dog – could have indefinitely for £85 per week. It should have been quadruple that amount so I snapped his hand off.

I soon had a great scam at the hotel, supplying the waiter and the barman with match tickets whenever they wanted them in return for free food and drink! I would end up playing my best football for Liverpool while I was at the hotel because I loved living there and had everything I needed.

I was right in the heart of the city so everything was close to hand and I could take Clyde out for his walk – even if there was once occasion Clyde escaped and ended up in the swimming pool! I stayed there for the best part of six months and it was a really happy time for me, but we couldn't live there forever. We eventually found a quirky place with a clock tower that was on a hill in Heswall Village.

Scoring goals makes the world a happier place and I was relaxed and playing well. There was good banter among the lads and great camaraderie. With characters like Bruce Grobbelaar around, there was rarely a dull moment.

He was at Anfield throughout my stay and I always thought he was a terrific goalkeeper. He was larger than life and unique in many ways, both on and off the pitch. He made mistakes like any keeper but, because he played for Liverpool, they were highlighted that much more.

He did things that no other keeper would even dream of and wasn't one for playing it safe. I lost count of the amount of crosses he came for and had no right to win – but did. He always put an element of doubt into the minds of the opposition attackers, who never knew what he would try next.

When Bruce made his mind up to go and collect, one of us would try to drop back on to the line in case things went wrong, but, more often than not, he'd snatch the ball out of the air like a cat.

The flipside was his mad moments and I remember one time early in my Liverpool career when I was somehow blamed for one of his rushes of blood. I can accept a bollocking as well as the next man if I feel it's fair, but I'm not sure it was merited on this occasion.

We were playing at home to Sheffield Wednesday and I lost possession in the D outside the Wednesday penalty area. The ball was cleared up into our half where Bruce had run way out of his box to clear. He was never getting anywhere near it and Imre Varadi simply knocked it to the side of him and passed the ball into the net from about 40 yards away.

Kenny was raging at me on the touchline for losing possession, but nobody said a word to Bruce. The ball had gone past a lot of people before it ended up in our net, but it seemed to be accepted that it was just one of those 'Bruce moments' that he was prone to every now and then.

He was an extrovert – some might say a show-off – and he had a short fuse too, as I discovered on a night out one time. We'd been to The Golden Egg Awards in London hosted by Noel Edmonds and had all been introduced to Virgin boss Richard Branson in the Green Room afterwards.

Branson invited us up to his club in Kensington so we agreed we'd go to The Roof Garden Club a bit later on. We went back to our hotel first and had a few drinks at the bar prior to setting off for a night out. There were a few girls sat chatting with us while Bruce held court, spinning off one or two yarns.

He had a big cigar in the corner of his mouth that he kept going to light but never quite got around to it, so eventually I said, 'One day you're gonna light that thing up, Bruce.'

As harmless a remark as it was, I could see he was a little irritated with me. We were always taking the piss out of each other so it was nothing unusual, but as we left, I slapped him playfully on the back of the neck to get a rise and he just flipped.

He grabbed hold of me and ran me into the toilet but, though he was trying to take a swing at me, I had hold of his wrists, trying to reduce the impact. John Wark was pulling Bruce back and telling him to calm down but to no avail – Bruce's head had gone by that stage. Because we'd had a few drinks, I was laughing to myself, which only made him lose the plot even more.

While I still had hold of his wrists, I said, 'Bruce, if you don't stop I'm going to have to knock you out.' He still managed to take a swing despite me holding his wrists and caught me in the eye with a wild swing. It eventually calmed down, we headed off for the club and by the morning I had a shiner to show for our evening on the tiles.

Back on the field, my relationship with Kenny had its prickly moments but my form meant I was an automatic choice and I doubt he'd have ever dropped me for personal reasons anyway.

I'd been on a fantastic run that had now seen me score 18 goals in 25 games and was in the form of my life, but Kenny was always in the background, looking for an opportunity to come on. Or at least that's how it felt.

The only thing I had on Kenny was age and the fact he didn't have the legs to play every game – but he still loved to play. It was almost always me he took off when he came on for the last 10 or 15 minutes. I suppose it was the best motivation any striker could have seeing Kenny warming up on the touchline, because invariably I'd up my game as a result.

I was linking up really well with Ian Rush in attack and probably heading for 20 or 25 goals that season, which would easily have been the best of my career at that stage. But just as everything had fallen into place, it then fell apart and I'd never get back to where I'd worked so hard to reach.

We were playing Manchester United in early February at Anfield and I had no idea that my season was about to come to an abrupt end as I went up for a header with Kevin Moran. My foot was in mid-air as we jumped, his leg crossed mine, trapping me so that when we landed I fell to the ground awkwardly. I felt an immediate bolt of pain in my ankle.

It felt like a bad one and later I'd discover that I'd ruptured my ankle ligaments. I was lay in some considerable discomfort as Roy Evans ran on, slapped a cold sponge and started to work it around on my ankle. I winced and said, 'Roy, for fuck's sake that ain't going to help, mate.'

John Wark came on in my place while I hobbled back to the dressing room, gutted. After an initial examination, Roy arranged for me to see the surgeon, Dick Calver. I had no idea how long I'd be out for. Though I was certain my ankle was knackered, I was still hoping against hope that it wasn't as serious as it felt.

Initially, Calver advised me to rest for few weeks, during which time I would receive treatment while slowly building the ankle's strength up. I went away thinking maybe I'd been lucky but there was only a slight improvement during that time.

Of course, you trust surgeons and doctors to know what they're doing, so I didn't really question the prognosis. But even after six weeks I was still miles off being fully fit. The truth was, nobody knew exactly what was wrong with my ankle because it hadn't been thoroughly investigated.

I'd had an X-ray but that only showed that there were no breaks or fractures and the general assumption was it was minor ligament damage which would eventually heal on its own. Nobody considered that if I returned to action too soon, it could set me back months.

Champing at the bit, I was desperate to move forward because it felt like nothing had changed since the original injury. So in late March, the next logical step was to have a run out for the reserves and see how things stood.

I was included in the team travelling to Hull, hoping for the best. I scored in a 3-1 win, but I was still feeling the injury, which was sore and stiffened up afterwards.

Being a midweek game, we got back into Liverpool at a reasonable hour and Sammy Lee, a big burly centre-back called John McGregor, John Durnin, Ken DeMange and I decided we'd go out to Chinatown for a meal and a few beers as we were off the next day.

We weren't going to have a heavy night so we nipped into the Coconut Grove for an hour and had a few drinks and a few laughs. There were a few scallies in there and, at that time of night and with a few drinks down them, they were potentially going to be a problem for us.

I noticed them glancing across at us and muttering to each other. Inevitably, they got a bit mouthy, but nothing we hadn't heard before and to be honest it was all water off a duck's back.

We paid up and left. McGregor and I got in a taxi to go on to Chinatown but Sammy was a minute or so behind. We waited in the taxi, but as I glanced behind, I saw this burly guy who'd been in the Coconut Grove was now giving Sammy shit on the corner. The scallies had followed us out.

McGregor wound the window down and we heard the guy say, 'You fat little twat!' in Sammy's face. McGregor said, 'Fuck it. I'm not having that,' and got out. He walked over to the big guy, got hold of him and punched him in the face.

I followed him over in case he needed a hand. From behind, somebody jumped on my back so I threw him off and booted him with my bad ankle – not the wisest thing I'd done A jolt of pain shot up my leg, but of course, you don't think about stuff like that in the heat of the moment.

It was nothing more than a scuffle in reality – John had banged the guy a couple of times but he'd been looking for trouble and as far as we were concerned, he'd got what he deserved and that was the end of it.

A day later, we went in for training as usual and two black Marias turned up – there were police everywhere. Sammy, John and I were all arrested and taken down to Tuebrook Police Station where we were all interviewed before being released in the afternoon.

Now we had a Crown Court case hanging over us, with all three of us accused of GBH. It was nuts as it was all self-defence at worst – maybe John's wasn't exactly, but had he not stepped in, Sammy might have ended up getting hurt. So he'd just dealt with a few dickheads that had been looking for trouble – it was them who had provoked it all in the first place.

We would have to prove our innocence in court at a later date but it was the last thing any of us needed. We all knew if things didn't go our way, we could be facing a jail term.

The club were obviously aware of the situation and said they would be standing by us. Because of that, we knew we'd have a decent legal team to argue our case. I put the whole situation out of my mind as best I could.

There was a heavy boozing culture at Liverpool and I was probably drinking more than I should have been. I can't think of anyone at the club who didn't enjoy a beer – some more than others – but that's how it was back then. It never stopped us working hard because we had high standards and we knew what was expected once you pulled on a Liverpool shirt.

DOUBLE WHAMMY

On some Tuesdays after training, we'd have a bit of a team bonding session and start off at a pub outside the ground by the Anfield Road End. We'd have a few beers and after a while, a few of the lads who were married or older would go home while the hardcore ones would carry on all day and maybe have a pool competition. Then a few more of us might go for a Chinese then off to a nightclub.

The Continental was our usual destination and Tuesday was the best night of the week because it was always rammed out.

Wednesday would usually be a day off if we had no midweek game, so we knew we'd be able to rest up and recover and maybe go for a game of golf the next day. With such regular contact with punters and with plenty of alcohol consumed, incidents such as the fracas outside the Coconut Grove were inevitable.

Kenny clearly held nothing against my involvement because my goal against Hull reserves convinced him that I was now ready to play for the first team again. At best it was a gamble and at worst it was a huge risk.

My ankle was still really sore but he wanted me to play against Sheffield Wednesday at the weekend. Even though I felt a million miles away from being ready, I said I would give it a go. 'Wee man, wee man,' he said. 'Just give me an hour, come on.'

I knew he was knackered because he'd played quite a few games on the bounce and needed a rest, but I was suspicious that there was another motivation to get me on the pitch and that it was more bonus-related. When you are injured in the first team, you still receive the win bonuses until you are available for selection. At £125 per point, it made a massive difference to your pay packet at the time.

The problem was, as soon as I set foot onto the pitch, I was obviously deemed fit. I wanted to play as much as anyone but by making myself available, I'd actually made things worse.

I lasted 60 minutes against Sheffield Wednesday and scored a couple more goals for the reserves the following week but the ankle worsened and I set myself back several more weeks.

My bonus payments stopped, which pissed me off no end. I'd known I wasn't fit enough to play in the first place and should have told Kenny as much. My own willingness to do what I could for the club despite the pain had now left me out of pocket as well.

I was gutted. I'd been stopped in my tracks and I knew my season was effectively over. I'd been enjoying the best run of my career before the United game and was one of the most in-form strikers in the country, but my ankle was so bad now I could hardly walk.

I would end up missing the FA Cup final, which would have been one of the biggest games of my career – the sort of match you dream of as a kid that makes all the hard work worthwhile. I'd also have no chance of being fit for the run-in.

I travelled down with the rest of the squad and watched the FA Cup semi-final against Southampton. Though I know it's selfish, I felt sick just watching it all happen in front of my eyes as we went on to win 2-0 in extra-time.

I knew that had my injury been correctly diagnosed straight away, I would have had a chance of being back for the last few weeks of the season. We beat Chelsea 1-0 on the final day to secure the league title at Stamford Bridge, with Kenny's chest and volleyed goal one of the most iconic Liverpool moments of recent times.

I doubt he'd have played even 15 games that season if I'd been fit, but people still remember that goal as the title clincher while my contribution towards that moment was largely forgotten.

Then we beat Everton 3-1 in the FA Cup final a week later to clinch the double. I'd been robbed of what would have been, at that point, the best moments of my career. Playing in the FA Cup final was something I'd dreamed about as a kid and I wasn't sure I'd get another opportunity.

It may sound as though I only cared about myself, but I'm just being totally honest and I can't believe anyone would feel differently. If they say they would, I think they'd be lying.

I watched the final from the bench, tracksuited up but no more than part of the backroom staff. After the game I had my picture taken on the pitch during the post-match celebrations, trying to look happy but feeling completely detached from everything. We had a reception in Covent Garden and then went to Stringfellows along with the FA Cup for a few beers. I drowned my sorrows.

There was one small consolation, however. I found out I'd been named in the PFA Team of the Season, which was satisfying because the votes had come from the players I played against week in, week out.

I was in good company too with Peter Shilton in goal plus Gary Stevens and Kenny Sansom as full-backs; Paul McGrath and Mark Lawrenson were the central defenders with a midfield of Glenn Hoddle, Bryan Robson and Stuart Robson and a forward three of myself, Gary Lineker and Mark Hughes.

I was quite proud that I'd been chosen because I'd been out for a few months, but my peers had still thought I was worthy of a place in the team of the year. It meant a lot.

I would have preferred to have walked out at Wembley and

played in a cup final but it hadn't been scripted. I needed to get my head together, get fit and come back again for the 1986/87 season. Well, that's what should have happened…

11

Walking Through a Storm

It was hard to believe a club the size of Liverpool had such amateurish medical practices. My ankle was no better by the time I returned for pre-season training and with training pitches harder than ever because of the hot, dry weather, I could barely run and was still limping badly.

I was finally booked in to see Dick Calver again and this time he suggested I should have an arthrogram to see what the problem was – something that should have been done several months earlier. I had the procedure, which basically injects a dye into the hollow below your ankle followed by an X-ray. If there are any tears, the X-ray will show where the dye is leaking out. It showed on the image that my ankle was leaking in three places. Calver looked at the X-ray plate and said, 'You need an operation, Paul' and I just thought, 'Why the fuck didn't you do that four months ago?' It was laughable.

I had the operation not long after, but it meant I had to miss pre-season yet again – the second year in a row that had happened to my cost. I would need a period of rehab to get back to where I needed to be, but I'd lost all confidence in the club's medical practices. The treatment room was a fair reflection of where Liverpool were at back then.

It was like a museum, with a wax bath and a load of rickety, archaic equipment. The rules were lax, too and they didn't mind if you took a cup of tea in there or read a paper. I'd been at other clubs where the last thing they wanted was for a player to feel comfortable in there – they wanted you out and back on the pitch.

On one occasion, Ronnie Moran was treating my ankle with an ultrasound machine and all of a sudden I could feel he was halfway up my shin. I looked at him and he was reading the back page of the paper, lost in his own world. I said, 'Er, Ron, the ankle's a bit lower down, mate.'

'It's your fault, you little cunt for bringing the paper in here in the first place!' he said making out I was in the wrong.

It is funny looking back but it gives you an idea of how things were at the time – and it got worse.

I was in the treatment room a few days later – bear in mind I'd been having ultrasound for several months by that point – when a guy came in to test all the equipment. After a simple procedure on the ultrasound machine, he informed us it wasn't even working! I'd been having treatment all that time and the fucking machine was broken. Christ knows how long it had been like that. I just shook my head but, by that point, I wasn't surprised and almost expected it.

I'd completely lost faith in the club's ability to rehabilitate me because nobody seemed to have a clue what they were doing.

I didn't have much of a build-up towards a return to the first-team but at least my ankle felt good again for the first time in a long while. I was fast-tracked back into the senior side with just a friendly against Blackburn Rovers and a game with the youth team before I was handed an unexpected chance to play again at the end of September.

I'd travelled to Goodison Park for the second leg of the Screen Sport Super Cup against Everton, which was a second-rate competition organised due to the lack of European football for English clubs. It was an all-Merseyside final, which had a modicum of interest to the paying punters, but not much more – how could you replace the European Cup?

We'd won the first leg 3-1 at Anfield and though I wasn't even in the squad, I was in the Goodison dressing room before the game when Kenny asked if I fancied a place on the bench. I told him I'd love to – my ankle felt fine and I was desperate to get going again.

Somebody had gone down with a stomach bug but I wasn't complaining and, with ten minutes or so to go, we were 3-1 up and I got the nod to come on for Steve McMahon. Kenny told me to go and enjoy myself for a few minutes.

I went on a little run with the ball and though my legs were a bit jellied up due to a lack of match action, it still felt good to be back – but my luck was running on empty. I went up for an aerial challenge and fell awkwardly, putting my arm down to break my fall. I felt a jab of pain straight away and after the game I told Roy Evans my arm was killing me. He said, 'Fuck off you soft shite. You've just been out for five months.'

I shrugged and left it at that. The next day I came in for training having not slept all night due to the pain. I was holding my arm close to my body throughout the session because of the pain. Roy finally told me I'd better get myself off to the hospital and I was thinking 'cheers!'

Seeing as there were no offers to take me, I set off driving in my (manual) car and made the best of it. The X-ray showed I had a fractured scaphoid, which is in the 'snuffbox' at the back of your hand.

They put a full plaster cast up to underneath my armpit, meaning I wasn't even allowed to train for two weeks. I couldn't believe my injury jinx had struck again.

I was allowed to play when the cast was cut to half the size, with the plaster ending across my knuckle meaning.

This meant I had to seek the referee's approval before I played – it also was a risk because I couldn't move my fingers due to the way the cast had been fixed. If I fell on them, I'd break them all if I landed badly. With my track record, it wasn't worth the risk. I couldn't stop a fall with my arm, so every time I went down I'd need to roll over like a stuntman to cushion the blow.

As soon as I was over my latest setback, Kenny lobbed me straight back into the first team away to Luton Town in late October. I wasn't match-fit but again I was just so happy to be back playing. The adrenaline was flowing and I played pretty well, even though we lost that game 4-1 on the plastic pitch.

My next game turned out much better as we beat Norwich City 6-2 at Anfield and I scored a hat-trick – complete with the plaster-cast. Then I played really well again in a 3-1 win over QPR. I'd done okay – I'd arguably been the man-of-the-match in all three games – but had no real fitness to carry me forward.

It was just the elation of playing again and enthusiasm and energy that had papered over the cracks. So by the fourth game, I was already starting to feel tired and jaded but after Kenny, Rushy and me, there was nobody deemed up to the job.

I'd needed to be eased back in to build up my fitness steadily but instead of being allowed to recover and get fully fit, I had to hit the ground running. I'd missed two pre-seasons in a row and the fatigue was becoming more evident each game.

Although I started the next 12 games, I didn't score once. I'd played 15 games on the bounce but they couldn't see I needed to be rested. We just didn't have the players to come in and cover so I had to carry on. I was aware that a few of the fans were moaning about my lack of goals and Kenny was saying we needed another striker. To be fair, we did need someone.

It was wrong to rely on Ian Rush, a half-fit Paul Walsh and an ageing Kenny Dalglish, who had all but phased himself out by that point. Had I been brought back in a controlled manner, I would have been fine, but instead Liverpool signed John Aldridge, who many thought wouldn't be a good partner for Rush because he was too similar.

Aldo wasn't a technically gifted player, but he was good at was putting the ball in the back of the net. Rushy and John actually clicked well and scored plenty of goals together.

I wasn't frozen out of the team completely but my involvement became more sporadic. One high-profile game I did play in was in the first leg of the Littlewoods Cup semi-final against Southampton at The Dell in February 1987. It was a bad-tempered game and I was in a frustrated state of mind because the goals had dried up for me. So when I got the ball from a throw-in and was clattered from behind by Kevin Bond – who stuck his studs right down my back for good measure – I wasn't best pleased.

We had a bit of a grapple but no more as I backed into him and though it was handbags at that point, he crossed the line when he leant in and spat in my face. I checked to see that the ref wasn't looking and then turned around and smashed him as hard as I could in the face. What I hadn't noticed in my eagerness to plant one on him was the linesman, who was stood about five yards away and saw the whole thing.

Bond went down and I didn't have a leg to stand on. I was sent off and I was waiting for my bollocking in the dressing room when Kenny walked in after the final whistle. We'd drawn 0-0 and he said, 'Wee man, you know you were wrong don't you?' I nodded, waiting for the inevitable, then he said, 'But if there's one person I don't mind you smacking, it's that twat.'

I felt I did well whenever I did get a chance, though Rushy and Aldo were now the preferred front pairing and I was left to wonder what might have been had my injuries been handled properly from the start.

We were going well in the league where we were in pole position going into spring and also had reached the Littlewoods Cup final after beating Southampton 3-0 at Anfield. But we hit a bad patch at the wrong time and lost three on the bounce in the league and then were beaten 2-1 in the final at Wembley by Arsenal. That was a game in which Ian Rush scored and Liverpool lost – the first time that had happened.

I played 73 minutes and had been picked because Aldo was

cup tied but when I saw Kenny warming up, I knew he was going to throw himself on for one last time at my expense, and that's exactly what happened.

It wasn't the fairytale end he'd hoped for as ten minutes later my former agent stablemate Charlie Nicholas slightly mis-hit his shot and as Ronnie Whelan dashed to get back, the ball struck him, diverting past Bruce Grobbelaar for the winner.

I was getting frustrated with the way things had been going and I still had the court case hanging over me, but that was finally about to take place after months of waiting. The trial actually started towards the end of the 1986/87 season and because it was Liverpool, the case was big news.

We had to face reporters and TV cameras on a daily basis and it wasn't a pleasant experience for any of us – not to mention the way it put the club's name in a bad light. After five days in court, we were told it would continue into the following week.

The season was nearly over and Everton had already wrapped up the title, so there was hardly a feelgood factor around the club as it was. After we finished at court on Friday, I received a call saying I was to join the rest of the squad at the team hotel for the game at Coventry the following day.

I'd read in the papers that Rushy was injured and a few others were struggling so I drove down to Coventry in preparation for the game and hoping to put the court case out of my mind for a few days.

On Saturday, I was on the coach to the ground and was just excited to be part of the team again – it had felt like an eternity since I'd been involved. Gary Ablett, God bless him, was there that day. He was only a 21-year-old kid with a couple of appearances under his belt so I figured I'd be starting or, with one or two bodies missing, at least be on the bench. But when Kenny told us who was playing, I wasn't even a substitute. I couldn't work out why he'd bothered to ask me to come down if he'd had no intention of playing me. Rushy had played and Aldo came on as sub but I just felt embarrassed.

I was already stressed out to fuck and was sick of Dalglish and his ways, so I wanted out. For whatever reason, I felt as though I was being treated differently.

I was furious and headed back to the hotel, got in my car and began the drive back up the M6, thinking, 'You Scottish fucking tosser,' as I sped towards home.

I was lost in my thoughts and, inevitably, paid no attention to the speed I'd been doing. I got pulled over by the police near Staffordshire, which led to a six-month driving ban. At that point, if there'd been a hole in the middle of the motorway I'd have happily driven into it.

The only positive note was that, a week later, we were rightly cleared in court of any wrongdoing during the Chinatown incident, which meant we could put the whole episode behind us once and for all.

It was a massive relief but the jury could see the witnesses testifying against us had been nothing more than opportunistic scallywags. They could see the way the whole thing had developed and agreed we'd been goaded and targeted.

Liverpool finished as runners-up in the league, some nine points behind Everton, so it was a disappointing end to what had been a promising season and not the ideal way to follow up the league and FA Cup double of the previous campaign.

I'd played 32 times in total – the majority of them from the bench – and scored six goals.

WALKING THROUGH A STORM

The fitness issues had taken their toll and I was a long way from being pleased with my overall contribution, though there had been mitigating circumstances. I had felt more and more as though I was being pushed towards the door and when Kenny brought in John Barnes and Peter Beardsley during the close season, I saw it that it was basically the end for me at Anfield.

Perhaps I had been too stubborn at times – I recall Roy Evans asking me once if I could play on the right as an attacking midfielder, but I was more pissed off that Kenny hadn't asked me – why didn't he just say he wanted me to play down the right?

I told Roy I wasn't interested and that I was a forward, not a winger, but in hindsight, I should have just done it. I'd played there for other clubs and I would have done a decent job and who knows where it might have led?

Maybe I was my own worst enemy on some occasions and not accepting that opportunity is a regret of mine, as it could potentially have worked well for me.

I should have moved on that summer, but for whatever reason, I was still a Liverpool player by the time the 1987/88 campaign began. It was in the final year of my contract in what would be my last season at Anfield.

Despite everything that had happened to convince me I was surplus to requirements, I came back still determined to fight for my place. When I'd moved to the club in 1984, it was accepted that if you were in the team and playing well, you'd keep your place, but Kenny didn't quite work to those rules.

Beardsley took a few months to find any real form but Kenny persevered with him even when he was clearly struggling. For me, there was no way back – even when I'd come in and done well I would be dropped once other options became available again.

I believe if I had been given another chance, I would have grasped it and kept Beardsley out of the side, but he was given long enough to turn things around and, to be fair, he became a top player for Liverpool. The truth was Kenny fancied Peter more than me. He was his signing and therefore he was prepared to be patient and prove his judgement had been spot-on.

That was disappointing because I felt I still had plenty to give and with a run of games, who knows what might have happened? You need competition at a big club and you need to know that if you're not performing, someone else will come and have their chance.

You need the person who has been left out to be pissed off and desperate to prove a point – had Kenny seen that in me, maybe things would have panned out differently for all of us.

I made the odd appearance off the bench here and there but it didn't take a genius to work out that the preferred front two would now be Rush and Beardsley. Aldo was also having his nose put out of joint by now, which in turn meant I'd slipped even further down the pecking order.

Kenny was still including me in every squad, taking me to every away game, but I wasn't even making the bench anymore.

I was travelling, staying at hotels and training but I wasn't getting a sniff so I was pretty demoralised with the whole situation. The end result was that because I knew I wouldn't be playing, I started to drink more and more at away games.

Once the manager had delivered the predictable news that I was not involved, I'd go to the bar and have a few beers, get on the coach half-pissed after the game and start making sarcastic comments on the way back trying to cheerful myself up – and then I'd go out again when I got home.

The only thing I was interested in by that point was getting pissed and enjoying myself because I felt I had nothing else to look forward to. I spent the best part of a year in that frame of mind, feeling sorry for myself and handling the situation badly.

On the medical side, there were too many people doing jobs they weren't qualified to do. I'm not blaming them but now my career at Liverpool, the move I'd dreamed of as a kid, was coming to a distinctly average end.

I'd become sloppy and unprofessional, but fitness-wise there were no issues because I was playing for the reserves each week – my main problem was a lack of focus.

I'd become disillusioned with everything and stopped doing the things that had got me to a top club in the first place.

That's what being frozen out can do to you if you handle it badly – when you turn up for training knowing that nothing you do will make any difference to the situation, your focus drifts and you all but give up. There's only so much you can do.

Demotivated, I found other things to occupy my time. I'd been in a bad place where I wasn't getting anything out of training any more so I was, in effect, waiting for someone to come in with an offer.

I'd allowed myself to become weak mentally, consoling myself by enjoying my social life more than my football and allowing that to compensate for what I wasn't getting on a Saturday afternoon.

Nothing gave me a buzz anymore and I missed playing in front of a big crowd and feeding off the atmosphere.

One thing I can say is that, from a pride point of view, I still gave it my all whenever I represented Liverpool, whether that meant giving 100% to Phil Thompson whenever I played for his reserve team or if I had a couple of minutes off the bench for the first team.

I knew that it was important to keep up my standards when I did play. If I was going to earn a move away, people would be judging my attitude and effort, particularly at reserve-team level.

I liked Phil and I also wanted to do myself justice, but my life away from the pitch meant I was contradicting my own values. I'd split up with Melissa as well, and started seeing Jane King, the daughter of former Tranmere manager Johnny King, who was a really nice girl as well.

My main problem was I had nobody to reinforce what I already knew – the way I was living was wrong.

There was one occasion when I did let Phil down, however, even though it was entirely unintentional. I was banned from driving at the time and relied on Nigel Spackman to bring me to and from training and games because he lived in the next village down.

We were due to play Everton in the reserve derby, which is still a big game on Merseyside and mattered to the fans and the players. I was living alone so I got up early and was planning the day out – I wanted to get my preparation just right.

I walked down to a nearby hotel to have a proper pre-match meal and was sitting there with my toast, egg and beans for lunch. I glanced at my watch and still had plenty of time. It was about 1pm when I headed back home to wait for Spackers when it suddenly dawned on me it was a 2pm kick-off and not 3pm. For fuck's sake.

I called Goodison Park and got hold of Thommo and explained what had happened, but he had the right hump and wasn't having any of it. He told me not to bother coming before hanging up.

When it got back to Kenny, he probably thought I'd been taking the piss, but I'd been trying to do everything by the book and had got it all wrong. It just about summed up the way things were going for me at that time where I just couldn't do anything right. It made me realise that the longer I stayed at Liverpool, the more damage I would do to my career.

Then, finally, my chance to move on and start afresh arrived. In February 1988, I got a call from Kenny. Nice as pie he says, 'We've agreed a fee with Tottenham, do you want to go?'

It wasn't a difficult decision to make – a chance to end my Anfield misery and a return to London – and that was that.

I said I was more than happy to move on and with that I was on my way back home and my time with Liverpool was over.

Looking back, things never quite fell into place for me at Anfield. It's a fantastic club with great supporters and I loved living in the city but, apart from the first couple of years, the rest of my time at Anfield was a bit of a nightmare.

It's all ifs and buts but had I not got injured when I did, I think I would have gone from strength to strength and scored a lot more goals and helped Liverpool win more trophies. At least I could say I went there and gave it my all, even if things didn't quite work out. I hope the fans have good memories of my time on Merseyside.

Now I had a new challenge back on my own patch. I wasn't sure what my old man would make of me playing for Spurs, but I'd be starting with a blank canvas and this was my opportunity to get my career back on track. I had no idea that moving to White Hart Lane would see my downward spiral continue as I went from one bad situation into another – one that, in many ways, was even worse…

12

White Hart Pain

Terry Venables was the manager at Spurs, he wanted me to play for him and that was good enough for me at the time. Terry had a reputation as a good man-manager and an excellent coach who liked his teams to play attractive and entertaining football. I'd thrived under a similar philosophy at Luton Town and I thought I could possibly rediscover my best form with Spurs and get back to where I wanted to be.

I had only recently turned 25 with perhaps my best years still to come, so on paper the move to White Hart Lane ticked all the right boxes. It would mean I was moving back to London and playing for another big club though, in truth, when you leave Liverpool, there are only a few clubs in the world that you could say were bigger – particularly during the Seventies and Eighties. It was never going to be a step up in that respect. The prospect of playing in my home city excited me and I was going to be near my family again so everything made sense, but it didn't take me long to realise that I actually missed living in the north.

To discuss terms, length of contract and the finer points of the move, I travelled down to the Royal Garden Hotel in Kensington and met up with Venables and my agent Eric Hall. We chatted and knocked around a few figures that weren't much more than I was on at Liverpool, but for that time, it was still decent money so with all parties happy, the deal progressed smoothly.

When everything was in place, the contract was drawn up and I signed the dotted line to become a Tottenham player on 16 February 1988. It wasn't hard to leave Liverpool because it was the right time to go. I needed to play games and my last match for the Reds – ironically a 2-0 win away to Spurs – had been almost three months earlier. I hadn't scored since banging one in after coming off the bench against Villa a year before.

I think my record of 37 goals in 92 starts – plus another 20 as sub – stands up and considering I was sold for £500,000, the four years' service had in effect cost Liverpool just £200,000.

The first thing Spurs did was to put me up in a five-star hotel with meals, drinks, laundry and phone calls all taken care of.

I was picked up for training every morning but I soon realised there wasn't the same winning mentality in the dressing room as there had been at Liverpool. There were a number of players who were either looking to move on or were on their way out of the club.

Clive Allen, a natural finisher who had scored 49 goals in his first full season, was soon leaving the Lane. I would have liked the chance to play alongside Clive a bit more, but as it was we only had three or four games together before he moved to Bordeaux.

I was match-rusty and it took me a few games to get going. I made my debut against Glenn Hoddle's Monaco in a friendly at White Hart Lane, losing 4-0 and then a few days later I was on the scoresheet in a 4-1 friendly loss at West Brom. Not the greatest of starts results-wise, but four days later I made my league debut in a 1-1 home draw with Manchester United.

We had some lively characters at the club and some good young players coming through as well. Vinny Samways, Neil Ruddock, John Moncur and David Howells were all emerging talents and needed guiding in the right direction, but I would discover as I went along that maybe Venables wasn't the right person to do that.

Our training ground at Ferguson's in Enfield wasn't the best for a club of Tottenham's size either. The pitches were soggy, the facilities weren't great and not what you'd expect of a top-flight side from London, so I was a bit underwhelmed by it all.

I'm not saying there was an unprofessional attitude through-out the club because we had players like Gary Mabbutt, who was the consummate pro. He played everything straight down the line and he had diabetes, so had to look after himself in every aspect of his life from training to his diet – almost to the point of irritation.

Chris Hughton was a gentleman and a great pro and Ossie Ardiles was also still at White Hart Lane at that point, though he was coming towards the end of his career. I'd grown up loving Ossie and watching the 1978 World Cup so it was a privilege and an honour to be at the same club as him. But apart from Ossie, Gary and Chris, there was an undercurrent among the squad that wasn't healthy and, to my own detriment, I soon became part of the problem.

Razor Ruddock was only 18 at the time but he was still a larger than life character even then. He'd come from Millwall and was revelling in his new life and the social scene that went with it. He was part of the group of lads that I started knocking around with.

Terry Fenwick, David Howells and Razor and I became pretty tight. We went off to Tenerife for a week on one occasion and Marbella for a few days another time as well as having plenty of lads' nights out in London.

The problem is, looking back, I remember times like that far more than most of the matches I played for Spurs, which is a sad indictment of my time with the club.

I was as much to blame as anyone for way we behaved and if anything, was one of the ring leaders, so I can't point the finger at anyone but myself. The fact was we wanted to enjoy ourselves more away from the pitch than on it.

Don't get me wrong, we weren't so poor we were fighting against the drop all the time, because we were there or thereabouts in the top six for most of the time – I just wonder how well we could have done had we had the focus and drive to be the best we could.

We knew we weren't as good as Liverpool or a couple of the other top teams and that we probably weren't good enough to win the league but we could have been better. On our day, we were capable of beating anyone. It's just those days were few and far between.

WHITE HART PAIN

Towards the end of the 1987/88 season we had Liverpool away – just two months after I'd left the club. I remember before the game not going out to warm up. I just didn't want to for whatever reason so I stayed in the dressing room.

Liverpool needed a point to win the title as they were 12 points clear of Manchester United with just four games to go so Anfield was rocking. I just wasn't sure what sort of reception I'd get so I stayed put, which was a shame.

When the lads came back from their knockabout on the pitch, they told me the Liverpool fans had all been singing my name and said it was unbelievable.

I was a bit choked up in truth but after they sang my name, they sang Peter Beardsley's – recognising the part I'd played at the club while showing they were right behind the player who was still there as well. It was a nice thing to do and when my name was read out before kick-off, I got another terrific ovation which again was nice.

I had an okay game and whether that was because of a lack of fitness, focus or a combination of both, I'm not sure – but we were well beaten on the day and the 1-0 win meant Liverpool were champions.

Looking back, it's funny how the final five fixtures fell for Spurs that season – Portsmouth, QPR, Liverpool, Charlton and Luton Town – meaning there were five of the six clubs other than Spurs I would play for in my career all in the space of a month.

The fact I didn't score a goal against any of them tells you a bit about where I was at, too. Though I found the net in a few friendly matches that were sprinkled in towards the end of the 1987/88 season, I wasn't happy with my return of one goal in my first 11 games for the club. We finished in thirteenth place so I'd hardly set the world on fire or got to anywhere near my best form.

I still believed I'd made the right decision and Spurs showed their ambition by bringing one of the most talented players in the English game to the club in the summer of 1988. Paul Gascoigne was signed from Newcastle United for a British record of £2.2m and if it had been a mad house before, it was about to go up a couple of notches on the cuckoo scale.

Venables brought in Paul Stewart from Manchester City and it would be me and Stewart who would be the chosen front pairing for the 1988/89 season. I think Spurs paid £1.7m for Stewie on the back of a great season with City, who were a second tier side at the time so, in that respect, he was still unproven in the top flight.

As for Gazza, there literally was never a dull moment. Because the club had a deal with the West Park Lodge Hotel I was staying at, they put Gazza in there as well. He was big news and had a press pack following his every move even in those early days.

The hotel was hardly a vibrant place to be and more like an old people's home, so you can imagine how things changed when Gazza arrived. He'd openly fart in front of everyone at breakfast and then just laugh it off – it was embarrassing if I'm honest but you'd still laugh in spite of yourself.

He was getting hounded by the paparazzi everywhere he went and it was starting to get out of hand, so the club shipped him down the road to another hotel where Paul Stewart, Nayim and a few other lads were staying. I was left in my hotel on my own and I'm fairly sure the club forgot I was staying there!

As a result, I'd bought a house just across the road from the hotel and with no pressure to move out, I was able to carry out renovations and build an extension while I stayed put at Spurs' expense.

About a year had passed before Venables came up to me a little agitated and said, 'You still in that hotel? You've been in there long enough – you've got a week to get out.'

With an uninspiring first few months under my belt with Spurs, I embarked on the 1988/89 campaign – my first full season with the club – looking to rediscover my old spark and enthusiasm.

On the opening day I played my best game yet for Spurs as we drew 2-2 at Newcastle United, getting a black eye from Kevin Scott after running him ragged on the day. Everyone was double-chuffed for me thinking, 'here we go – he's got himself fit and is finally on his way' – but in truth that was as good as it got and I wouldn't match that performance again that season.

The problem was my habits towards the end of my time at Liverpool had become so ingrained in me that I simply carried on the life I'd led for the previous year or so without treating it as fresh start. I'd get back on a Saturday evening and go out drinking until late and then go out again on Sunday looking for women. That's what my life was at that time in many ways.

I was single again and living the sort of life a young lad my age on decent money was expected to lead – the only issue was that it wasn't the life a professional footballer should lead.

I wasn't focused for the first few years in truth and I was running at about 70% of my capacity at best. I wasn't doing myself or the club justice.

For the talent we had at the club, we were fairly average all round and by early December of my first full season we'd won just three league matches out of 15 and were just five places off the foot of the table.

I still wasn't scoring with any regularity and the only reason we weren't bottom was the form of Gazza and Chris Waddle, who were creating and scoring most of our goals.

In fact Waddle enjoyed reminding me of something I'd said a few months earlier on our pre-season tour of Sweden where I'd done well and scored four goals in the first three friendlies.

I felt fit and sharp and I was chatting to a girl at a bar when she asked what my name was so I said, 'Paul's my name, goals are my game,' just having a laugh. Waddle, who was stood with me, had a chuckle too.

Of course, with just one league goal by early December, Waddle liked to remind me of that statement whenever he got the chance, especially as he was second top scorer by that point. I deserved it and would have done the same given the chance.

Thankfully, we started to improve around the festive period and began to climb the table, but there were still things that weren't right at the club. I remember us losing 1-0 to Bradford City in the FA Cup in January, which was embarrassing.

We had enough about us to have had a good go at the competition, but we'd been knocked out by a team who were a division below and it wasn't good enough.

We got on the coach afterwards to head back to London. There was a kitchen at the back with two waiters serving food and drink. They came and asked how we wanted our steak and whether our Chablis was chilled enough and I'm thinking, 'Fuck me, we've just been beaten by Bradford and we're being treated like kings.' It wasn't the way it should have been.

It just didn't feel right to be pampered with five-star treatment after playing shit. At Liverpool, no matter where we went, we always stopped off and got fish and chips on the way home and had a couple of crates of beer to wash it down with.

We'd eat it out of the paper with no airs and graces – and this was a team that was winning trophy after trophy, don't forget. Venables just wasn't a shouting and screaming manager, but there were occasions when you just wished he'd raise his voice and have a good go at us. That obviously wasn't how he operated.

I wasn't above it all looking down, taking the moral high ground. I was as much a part of the problem as anybody. But the fact we had a match on Saturday had become almost incidental, with the focus more on the next piss-up.

I felt unprofessional but couldn't rise above it and regenerate myself. Terry always said we were grown-ups so he was going to treat us like adults, but the problem is most footballers aren't grown-ups because they are privileged and act like kids.

At that point in my life, I needed a manager who was on top of me a bit more and took more of an interest in my private life to make sure I was doing the right things. I needed someone on my case a bit more and taking an interest in what I was up to outside of the club. That's where I was letting myself down – things might have been different had that happened.

I'm not blaming anyone else for the way I was behaving, that was down to me, but with a bit more discipline aimed in my direction I may have realised what I was doing was putting my career in jeopardy. The fact was that Tottenham were the right club for me – but it was the wrong time to be there.

One of the things that struck me as time went on was that Venables' guru-type reputation for being an unbelievable coach was something of a myth. He wasn't quite the football genius the press often painted him to be. The lack of professionalism from the majority of the squad seeped down from the relaxed way the club was run.

Having said that, there was without doubt an element of lads, myself included, who got over defeats very quickly because the emphasis for us after a game was more about where we were going to go out later that night. We were all grown men and professional footballers who should have known better.

So my life was unsettled on and off the pitch and now I had to leave the hotel. I was about to enter the lion's den where things could only go from bad to worse. My house was still two months away from completion so I asked Nayim if I could stay with him at the hotel he was at and he was fine about it. I moved my gear into the spare bed in this room and for the next two months it was pure bedlam.

Gazza, Jimmy Five Bellies and Paul Stewart, all in one hotel – it was never dull, let's just say that. You never knew what Gazza would get up to next so when he turned up with an air rifle one day, it was no great surprise. He'd try to shoot things from his window – rabbits, birds, static targets – or on one occasion a couple of hotel lights in the corridor outside his room.

Inevitably, he moved on to a larger target. On one occasion when he was pissed, Gazza offered Jimmy £50 if he'd let him shoot him in the back which, of course, Jimmy agreed to. He took his shirt off and Gazza fired the gun. Next thing Jimmy was rolling around in agony almost in tears while Gazza was rolling around crying tears of laughter.

Jimmy got up, looked in the mirror to see what his injury looked like, saw a big red mark and lay down crying again –

it was like that every day in one way or another. Jimmy was always game for a laugh, even if the laughs almost always came at his misfortune.

On another occasion we were in the hotel bar and Gazza was smoking this big cigar. He said to Jimmy, 'I'll give you £50 if I can hold this on the end of your nose for 10 seconds.'

Again, Jimmy accepted the challenge and everyone had to hold his arms out of the way and keep his head still while Gazza held the cigar in place with his mate screaming in pain. Even two months later Jimmy still had a big scab on the end of his nose.

There was another occasion when Gazza and I went to Guernsey to visit some disabled kids that turned into another rollercoaster ride into madness. A guy had asked me if Gazza would come over and I said I'd convince him so we arrived at the centre where there were some physically disabled kids, some with cerebral palsy and various other handicaps.

Typical of Gazza, as we walked in, he started pretending he was handicapped, walking awkwardly and so on. I was absolutely mortified to begin with but then he burst out laughing and started cuddling the kids and making them laugh with his usual antics. They all loved him but it was almost surreal how he got away with it. I thought the mums and dads would be disgusted but because it was Gazza and he was just being himself, he got away with it.

On the way back from Heathrow, we were both a bit hungry so we stopped at a Wimpy near the airport and both had double cheeseburger and chips. A kid in a car outside the window spotted Gazza and waved at him so he looked back, put the whole burger in his mouth and chewed it with his mouth open, making the kid and his family laugh. Gazza had wanted a 99 ice cream as well so when I'd paid the bill, the guy serving me had whipped up the biggest ice cream you've ever seen – because it was for Gazza.

I took it over and collected the change and by the time I got back to our table, the chocolate flake had gone and he had ice cream all over his nose and chin. He tidied himself up a bit and we got back into to the car where he continued to eat his 99.

We started driving up the road and about 100 yards ahead was a cyclist in the all-in-one shorts and top, helmet and an expensive looking bike. As I indicated to pull out, I noticed Gazza's window was lowering. As we passed, the cyclist looked to his right and Gazza launched what was left of his cone at him, hitting him in his right eye socket.

We drove on and we were both in tears, pissing ourselves as we pulled further away from this poor bloke. We were about 300 yards clear of him when I hit a line of cars stood at a red traffic light. I said to Gazza, 'That was absolutely brilliant, but that cyclist is pedalling like fuck and he doesn't look happy.'

Gazza started to think about what he'd done when the light changed, but because we were eight cars back, we still weren't moving and the cyclist was, by now, level with us. He threw his bike to the floor while Gazza put down the lock. The bloke started to kick fuck out of my door – just as the car in front started to move and I pulled away.

Gazza, all brave as a lion again, turned around and started waving two fingers at the cyclist who quickly fell out of sight and that was that. Just another day with Gazza!

Towards the end of my time at the hotel, I was glad to get out of what had become a mad-house because I'd had enough. It got to the stage where I was just thinking 'not again…' every time something happened.

It was relentless and, apart from Stewie, most of the lads were single. So there were endless shenanigans with various girls out for a good time and some of the female hotel staff, too.

The problem was that we would have breakfast, go to training, have some lunch and then you'd be back at the hotel for around 2pm – then what were you supposed to do? There were only so many times you could go to the hotel leisure club and there was not much else going on so invariably you'd end up getting into mischief.

There was many a time when you'd get back at various hours of the day and one of the lads would be otherwise engaged, shall we say. While it was all good fun, by the time I moved into my house, I'd had my fill of living like that and was craving some kind of normality again.

I suppose the unsettled, hectic lifestyle mirrored my performances on the pitch, which only occasionally hit the levels I should have been at consistently. I had fun and enjoyed myself, but from a professional point of view it was ridiculous in terms of the whole set-up and the lack of discipline.

Despite the circus that came with him, Gazza was great entertainment, daft as a brush and nothing more than a loveable rogue. I recall there was an opportunity for a trip in a helicopter to Brands Hatch so we dragged Gazza along, knowing that he had a bit of a fear of flying.

Before we got to our helicopter, the guy showing us around took us on a private jet for a quick nosey. It was obviously prepared to fly imminently because there was a big plate of sandwiches on the table. As Gazza was the last one off, he hung back a little and just bashed the plate with his fists until the food was all squashed together.

He was giggling to himself as we walked over to the helicopter and he said, 'They're going to get on there in a bit and find all their sandwiches mashed up – and that was me!'

And that pretty much summed up his child-like, almost innocent sense of humour. Once we got up in the air, the guy who owned the company was the pilot and Gazza started tugging his seat belt every now and then so it rose up high on his neck. Then he was sticking his hands out of the tiny window flaps at the side of us and trying to slap his head. He was just like a big kid up to mischief all the time.

As for his drinking, in the early days, I'm not even sure he liked a drink that much. He didn't drink to be sociable; he drank to get pissed as quickly as he could. When we were all at the same hotel, he'd get a pint of lager at the bar and put loads of other shit in it and then drink it all in one go. Then he'd be gone within 20 minutes, falling about like an idiot. I couldn't see the point of it but it was how he wanted to be.

There was an occasion when he came out with Steve Sedgley, Mitchell Thomas and me. We went to a top nightclub called Browns on Great Queen's Street in London, which was a bit of a footballer and celebrity hangout. They had a VIP bar upstairs that we all went up to and Gazza began going around picking everyone's drinks up and throwing them down his neck.

There were three or four black lads at the end of the bar and they knew who Gazza was. One of them came over and said, 'Look guys, we know who he is but he needs to slow up a bit.'

He could really embarrass you but he continued wandering around, drinking and talking absolute shit so we needed to get him home quickly, bringing the evening to a swift end. When we went outside there were paparazzi waiting. Seeing him in that state was exactly why they hung around for hours.

Gazza sold papers and he was playing right into their hands. Before we got in the car he was sick up against the window.

He was a funny lad and I don't know whether it was a confidence thing or whether the drink gave him Dutch courage or not – I suppose only Gazza knows why he drank like he did.

I have no opinion good or otherwise about his drinking habits and I'm certainly not going to start preaching about somebody else when for two or three years, I wasn't where I wanted to be.

I always smile when I think of him because he always did things back to front. He was paranoid about his weight and would often make himself sick before a game. There was one occasion where he played three sets of tennis the night before a cup match at Portsmouth.

He was a complex individual, vulnerable in many ways and he may have had an eating disorder of some kind, but he was basically a great lad. Like me, Spurs were a good club for him, but what he'd needed was a disciplined environment with a strong manager in charge – Tottenham had neither at that time.

I was still enjoying myself and living the life – just not the right life. Many of the other lads could go home to their wives and families after a night out but I had nobody to answer to so I just carried on.

I'm sure I wasn't flavour of the month in the Fenwick household as Terry was my partner in crime. We'd have many a good night at Browns, where George Michael, Elton John or any number of famous stars would sometimes be.

The only responsibility I had was being a professional footballer and that's something I wasn't handling very well. The whole of the 1988/89 season is just a blur in all honesty – there's nothing memorable about any of it apart from one game when I scored twice against Everton, curling a beauty past Neville Southall, who I always seemed to score goals for fun against. But other than that... nothing.

I just wasn't playing well, wasn't as fit as I should have been, had no focus and was playing at around two-thirds of my capacity. For the first 18 months of my time at White Hart Lane, I was a waste of space.

The beginning of the end of the cycle of drink, women and partying came when I'd been in a bar having lunch one day. Me and a few of the lads had a sort of end-of-season party planned for the evening. I'd noticed a woman in the bar and she was sitting with a couple of friends so I asked if they fancied coming along to the party later that evening and then back to my house for a few drinks with a load of other people.

Her name was Bev and we hit it off straight away. I don't think she had a clue that I was a footballer, which was something I liked. We started seeing each other not long after, though it was a slow-burner. I sort of resisted getting in too deep at first because I was having too much of a good time, but over a period of a few months we started getting a bit more serious. But I still wanted to have my cake and eat it, so I wasn't about to change overnight.

That said, I was desperate for some stability in my home life so meeting Bev was exactly what I needed. The question from a career perspective for me was whether or not it was too late to turn things around...

13

One Flew Over the Cuckoo's Nest

As a result of the lack of goals during my first full season at Spurs, Gary Lineker joined the club from Barcelona at the start of 1989/90 and it was Stewie who got the nod ahead of me to be his partner. Lineker was a natural goalscorer and he brought something to Spurs that had been missing. I think Johan Cruyff had been playing him as a right winger at Barcelona – something he never was going to be – and he'd taken the opportunity to come back to England.

Lineker was single-minded, selfish and was only concerned about scoring goals at that time. I always got the impression that he was one of those centre-forwards who would be happy if he scored, regardless of the result. That's not a criticism, just how he was. Maybe the best strikers are all like that deep down.

It was ironic that as Lineker arrived from Spain, I looked set to go in the opposite direction. John Toshack was manager at Real Sociedad at the time and I think his old mate Roy Evans at Liverpool might have recommended me. I was made aware of their interest and I was definitely up for the move, as a change of surroundings was probably just what I needed.

It was plastered all over the back pages for a few days as the new season was about to start and I told Bev that I might be off imminently. In fact, it turned out that the deal fell through for one reason or another, but I said to Bev that we'd better go for a drink to celebrate the move anyway! I let her mum know it was a wind-up but at the bar there was Champagne with balloons carrying good luck messages. At the end of the night I said, 'Nah, the move's off!'

Around that period I also got a call from Venables saying I could possibly move to Marseille if I was up for it, as part of the deal that would see Chris Waddle move to France.

I got quite excited about the move and fancied playing abroad because I thought the lifestyle would suit me, even though I'm not exactly sure where I would have fitted into a side that had Jean-Pierre Papin leading the line.

But I was confident that, given the chance, I'd fit into the playing style quickly. I would be valued at £800,000 and Chris was £4.2m – a lot of money at the time.

A couple of days passed before I went with Chris to Wimbledon with his mate Pat to watch a bit of tennis and enjoy the hospitality. We were having a laugh and enjoying the day when all of a sudden, Chris took a call, listening intently.

When he'd finished, he started throwing drinks down his neck for what I can only assume was because he'd just been told his move to France had been finalised. Then I got a call not long after to say I wasn't part of the deal anymore and everything was off. So Chris was elated and I was deflated!

I'll never know why the deal fell through or what might have happened had I gone and played in France for a couple of seasons. I regret that I never had a chance to play overseas, but that's the way my hand was dealt at the time. Marseille would have been a fantastic adventure.

I had demons to exorcise before I could justifiably say I should be playing again. I'd gone to Spurs weak and carried on being weak, preferring a good laugh because I didn't have the will, desire or whatever you want to call it to drag myself out of the downward spiral I'd been in at that stage of my career.

It was all about enjoying myself socially and being in London amplified the problem because there was that much more going on. Bev was proving a calming influence on me but I was still hanging on to my old life by my fingernails.

I still enjoyed the company of my team-mates and Paul Stewart was an expert piss-taker with a really dry sense of humour. The banter at Spurs was brutal at times and often a bit near the knuckle – much more than it had been at Liverpool – and sometimes got a bit out of hand.

There were rumours that Spurs were looking to sign Pat Van Den Hauwe from Everton and I was praying it wasn't true. I'd played against Van Den Hauwe during one or two Merseyside derbies and I just didn't like the guy.

I remember bumping into a mate of mine, Roy Wright, who used to do some odd jobs for me and a few of the lads when I was at Liverpool. He was a good bloke and a staunch Evertonian – he was in the Moat House Hotel bar having a drink with Graeme Sharp and Van Den Hauwe when I walked in.

John Barnes was with me at the bar so I went across to say hello. I didn't know Sharpey that well but he was a decent lad and I'd never spoken to Van Den Hauwe before so I was a bit taken aback when he said, 'I see you've brought your black cunt mate', nodding over at Barnsey across the bar.

I knew before Pat opened his mouth that I wasn't going to like him but now he had spoken, he'd confirmed he was a complete prick. I think he saw himself as some sort of tough guy, but he was stood there in a bright orange silk shirt, unbuttoned to halfway down his chest and looked a right tit.

I couldn't resist so I said, 'Your missus not going out tonight, then?' He asked me what I was talking about and I said, 'Isn't that her blouse you've got on?'

His arm came out to grab my neck and I slapped it away and said, 'Get to fuck,' and though it got silly for a few seconds, that was the end of it.

I told Barnsey what he'd said and he wanted to go and sort him out there and then. I should have let him.

I didn't have any contact with Van Den Hauwe after that incident – that was until Spurs actually bought him. After training and hearing the news, I remember telling all the lads what a dickhead we'd signed when in walks the man himself to say hello. Quick as a flash, Stewie turned to me and said, 'Walshy? You said Pat was a right wanker, didn't you? Didn't you say he was a dickhead and a tosser?'

It was typical Stewie and I suppose I'd asked for it. Van Den Hauwe didn't know what to do and just stood there for a few minutes with neither the intelligence nor the wit to respond. Spurs officially announced they'd signed him shortly after and he moved to Chislehurst, which is a nice part of south London. It wasn't too long before we realised he had one or two issues.

He used to come in for training, get showered and changed afterwards and then stay out all day. He'd find a bar and just stay in there until closing time.

I wasn't married to Bev at this stage but I was trying to get out of my old habits. Against my better judgement, there was one occasion where a few of us had been out and he was pissed up, so he asked to stay at my house.

I wondered if I really wanted him in my house at all but in the end, I let him sleep in the spare room and it confirmed what I already thought about him.

In my opinion, he was a fucking oddball. He was walking around the house mumbling to himself all the time like Dick Dastardly's dog Muttley. He just didn't seem a full shilling. Of course, we later found out there were a few other things going on in his life at the time.

On the pitch, while Stewie and me got on well, we had struggled as a strike partnership because neither of us were prolific goalscorers – it was just one of those things where we didn't gel.

We had Chris Waddle on the left providing crosses but when the chances did come along I didn't make the most of them – the truth is I was more bothered about how my fucking hair looked at that time.

Stewart had ended the 1988/89 with more than double my goals tally – I'd only scored six goals in 32 starts and I'd also made five appearances from the bench, so I had no cause for complaint. Venables had paid a lot of money for Stewie and was determined to make the signing a success, so persevered with him more than me. I wasn't giving him any reason to justify playing me, though I could blame nobody other than myself, having been given a fair crack during my first full season.

When I was at it, my game was all about making things happen, playing at a high tempo and working hard for the team. I should have been scoring at least 15 goals a season and creating chances for others, but the team had been suffering without a recognised finisher in the side.

You can get away with it if one of the strikers isn't finding the net while the other one is. But if you're both firing blanks, it's going to end badly for someone.

On paper, to have Waddle and Gazza in the team must look like a striker's dream, but despite Gazza's talent, he wasn't brilliant for forwards. He could do so much on his own that he didn't really need anyone else.

It's not a criticism, but he was young, had loads of energy and wanted to score goals himself – he could win games on his own and he was a real-life Roy of the Rovers in many ways. More often than not the best you'd get would be a one-two from him because he'd beat one, then another and then play it into you but want it straight back before going on to score.

He rarely played clever little threaded passes or put you through on goal because that wasn't his style. He was a fantastic player – pure class and without doubt one of the most naturally gifted footballers I ever played alongside – and he could mix ability with piss-taking like nobody else.

In the third game of the 89/90 season away to Man City, Paul Lake, an upcoming talent in his own right at the time, was getting the better of him in midfield and he didn't like it one bit.

If he felt someone else was in control or outshining him, he'd resort to mimicking them or trying to exact some form of public humiliation. Lakey was edging the battle at Maine Road so Gazza started pulling his ears out to mimic Lakey's ears and while it was playground stuff, it was funny as well – that's how he was.

He'd start standing on the ball and try to make his opponent look stupid – it was the price of outperforming Gazza and making him work harder to win the duel. He'd either do that or mug them off and make them look small in front of the crowd to get his own back.

He had a number of duels like that and usually won them – he scored our goal that day in a 1-1 draw so maybe that particular battle ended honours even.

Another time he broke his arm on the head of Coventry City's Lloyd McGrath after he'd given him a frustrating afternoon. If he singled you out for individual attention, it was a back-handed compliment from a very special footballer.

He had a great rapport with opposition fans too – even in the middle of a heated London derby at Upton Park – as he was tackled and then rolled over about seven times as if he was really injured. In reality, he was just taking the piss and jumped up, smiling at the West Ham fans, and they in turn were laughing back. I don't know many players who could have got away with that.

By the time we played Arsenal in October 1989, I'd scored just seven goals in 59 appearances since signing for Spurs and nobody had to tell me it was a piss-poor return. An injury to Paul Stewart gave me a rare start against the Gunners and I scored what would prove to be the winning goal in a 2-1 victory.

Unfortunately for me, it proved to be one of many false dawns and the next game, I was dropped again. I had to make do with the odd start here and there or be forced to come off the bench. I suppose I didn't take it too well because I felt I'd have forged a good understanding with Lineker, but we never had a decent run of games together. I was a long way from having a guaranteed a place in the starting XI but, by that point, I didn't deserve one.

As an example of how far I'd allowed my own standards to slip at Spurs, I went along to meet George Best, his girlfriend Mary Shatila and his agent Phil Hughes one day for what should have been a harmless lunchtime drink and a chat about any possible opportunities for George that a business associate Richard Mee was trying to get off the ground.

I was there in an introductory role more than anything. I had met George on Cilla Black's Surprise, Surprise! a few years earlier but didn't really know him that well. We'd been part of the same team who played against a group of lads who were thrashed every time they played, so a game was organised at Highbury to play them. Tom Finney, George and myself were involved and it had been a good laugh.

So we met at Pucci Pizza in Chelsea and going off the last training session I'd had, I was fairly sure I wouldn't be in the squad to face Wimbledon the next day. So Richard and I ordered a beer while George asked for a large glass of wine.

There was some commotion under the table which started to move a bit and I took that to be Mary shoving George and probably indicating for him not to drink – advice he'd ignored for most of his adult life. After he'd washed down a couple more, he was totally gone.

Despite his state, he was still up for some action and asked if we wanted to go and have a game of pool at a club in Mayfair, where we inevitably ended up having a few beers as well.

I drank much more than I should have done because even though it was unlikely, there was always a possibility I might be needed for the match the next day. I'd broken my own golden rule of not drinking on the days leading up to a game and it was about to come back and bite me on the arse.

The saddest part of the day for me, however, was watching George trying to line up a shot and seeing him unable to focus or co-ordinate properly. That is my abiding memory of a guy I'd grown up idolising as a kid.

As luck would have it, the next day I arrived at the ground to find out a couple of the lads had picked up injuries in training and there were also one or two who were ill. So not only had I been drafted into the squad, I was actually starting – I thought to myself, 'fuck me!'

It was just desserts I suppose as I was still recovering from a fairly heavy night out with George – not exactly the ideal pre-match preparation!

I had a ridiculous hangover, had drunk enough alcohol to probably be classed as half-cut and ended up being hauled off at half-time. I was hopeless, couldn't focus and a shambles for 45 minutes – and I'm embarrassed to admit as much.

I'd got exactly what I deserved but it was the first and only time I'd done that and a measure of how far I'd drifted in terms of professionalism. In many ways, that was as low as I sank at Spurs and I suppose it marked the end of two-and-a-half years of being a waste of space for both Liverpool and Tottenham.

I would have good games here and there when I did play, but

WALSHY

I couldn't get a lengthy run in the team and my goals return was still crap.

While I'd spent too long at the wrong end of the scale, Lineker was exactly the opposite. He was a top striker but he didn't like training – just playing and scoring goals.

He did the minimum he had to do because he was playing every week for Spurs and England and probably felt he was doing enough. He would have a laugh on the coach to and from games and had a good sense of humour, but he'd always keep himself to himself and go home afterwards rather than go out for a drink.

So though my style would have suited his well, I played second fiddle throughout my second full season with Spurs and it felt like Liverpool all over again. Lineker scored 26 goals in his first year and proved to be a great signing, while I was getting more and more frustrated with the situation.

However, with just three goals that season, again, I hadn't delivered. I played 31 times, but 18 of those had been off the bench and what I'd really needed was a run of six games or so to build momentum up.

At least my personal life was on the up and Bev and I tied the knot during the Italia '90 World Cup. That summer I watched on as my old mate Gazza became an international phenomenon before England went out in the semi-final to Germany.

14

A Series of
Unfortunate Events

Now a married man and feeling settled and happy for the first time in several years, I was finally training properly and living the way I was supposed to once again. There were far fewer all-day drinking sessions and fewer late nights but I still couldn't force my way back into the team.

The problem was, as we began the 1990/91 season, Gazza and Lineker were scoring regularly, the team were playing well and we were unbeaten in all competitions going into November, so there was no need to for Venables to consider other options. I had to wait until the 10th game in, a meaningless League Cup second leg against Hartlepool, for my first start.

We were already 5-0 up from the first leg but at least it was a run-out and with Lineker injured for the next game, I kept my place for the home match against Sheffield United. With eight league games gone, Stewie still hadn't scored, but he had notched both goals in the 2-1 cup win over Hartlepool. Spurs had only managed 11 goals in those eight league games, even though we sat in third in the table and were still unbeaten.

I was determined to make the most of it against Sheffield United and things couldn't have gone any better as I scored a hat-trick in a 4-0 win and made the other goal for Nayim. I thought that, with some justification, I'd finally earned an extended run and maybe I could get back on track again, but before our next game away to Nottingham Forest, Venables dropped a bombshell.

We were staying at the East Midlands Airport Hotel, where he pulled me to one side in the busy reception area to tell me I wasn't playing. Maybe he thought that because there were a lot of people milling around I would accept it quietly and get on with it. I just stood up, told him to fuck off and then left for the pub next to the hotel, where I sat and I drank five pints of lager, one after the other.

There's no doubt there were times when I was my own worst enemy, but I was fuming because I felt what he'd done was unjust. I think on this occasion I was right. Venables had suggested I'd only scored three against Sheffield United because they'd had a man sent off. I said to Venables, 'So it was only me playing against ten men, was it?' It wasn't the sort of motivation I was looking for, really.

To me it meant that no matter what I did, I would never get the run I needed in the team under Venables, whether I merited it or not. The next morning he asked if I would be one of the subs and, with nothing better to do, I agreed.

During the game, I remember warming up on the touchline when Brian Clough came out of his dug-out and gently moved me along, much to the crowd's amusement. I had to smile, too.

I eventually replaced Steve Sedgley in the second-half as we beat Forest 2-1 with two goals from David Howells, despite Stewie missing one or two good chances during the game. He had nothing to worry about though because his place was clearly never under threat.

Venables later tried to vindicate his selection by saying we'd won the game and he'd been proved right, but he'd been wrong to drop me – who drops a striker who has just scored three goals and made the other one? That's why I don't think he is quite the coaching genius he's often been portrayed as. It's not rocket science to carry on with somebody who has just hit form.

So, just like I'd become under Dalglish at Liverpool towards the end, I became cynical and pissed off because I felt no matter what I did, I wouldn't be picked.

For any footballer, that's a pretty miserable situation to be in, though again, I'd brought a lot of the problems on myself with my past misdemeanours.

We were still unbeaten when we played leaders Liverpool at White Hart Lane in early November, but had to beat them if we were going to be serious title contenders. I came on for Nayim but we were well beaten and lost 3-1 on the day. I scored off the bench against Wimbledon the following week but I was only getting 20 minutes here and there.

I'd miss a few games and then be back on the bench, so it was hard to get any rhythm going. But when I scored two off the bench against Sunderland a few weeks later, it meant that I'd scored six goals from just four starts, where Stewie had just five from 19. I'd done all I could, yet the pattern would continue throughout the season.

At least there was always Gazza around to keep me entertained. Italia '90 had made him a massive star and every day he'd receive a pile of fan mail, much of it from gorgeous women wearing very little and saying how they'd love to meet him.

I was at the training ground one time and he showed me a few of them. I asked him, 'Christ have you looked in the mirror lately? Tell them not to forget their white stick' and the usual banter. Let's face it, he wasn't blessed in the good looks department, but what he lacked in looks he more than made up for in personality. He loved the adulation and being ever the showman, he lapped it up.

Wimbledon may have had the Crazy Gang tag, but with characters like Van Den Hauwe, we weren't far behind. Add in Gazza, Ruddock, Stewart and one or two others including Steve Sedgley – who was a filthy, funny, dirty and farty smelly bastard – it wasn't hard to see why there was a lack of discipline at the club.

Venables was putting a bunch of clowns together and it was just a crazy time to be a Spurs player.

Then there was Terry Fenwick. The lads called him 'Son of Terry' because he'd followed the manager around quite a lot in his career and he was someone Venables clearly valued as a player. The lads would say after training, 'What are you and your dad having for tea tonight?'

All in all, it was an eclectic mix of talented, unruly rogues alongside model pros like Lineker, Hughton and Mabbutt.

A SERIES OF UNFORTUNATE EVENTS

We never reached the heights we were capable of because we should have been challenging for the title with the squad we had. Maybe we ran on 70-80%, occasionally raising our standards higher and blowing teams away, but mostly never fulfilling our true potential.

I remained a peripheral figure, playing here and there, but the goals had dried up. I remember losing my wedding ring on the pitch on one occasion and Dave Howells – who was witty, but one of the quieter members of the squad – told me not to bother looking in the penalty area. I found it amusing and would have said the same myself given half the chance.

There was one game during the 1990/91 season that still makes me smile, however. I was about to become a father for the first time and Bev was in hospital waiting to have our first child by caesarean section. She was booked in for 10am on 12 January 1991.

I'd also been included in the squad to face Arsenal in the derby later that day so as long as everything went well, I was hoping it was going to be a day to remember. I was at the hospital overnight and didn't get much sleep, but when Bev gave birth to Jordan on time, it was the most incredible feeling of my life. Holding my son for the first time is something I'll never forget.

Bev was tired and sore but in good spirits and we had plenty of family around, meaning I was good to join the rest of the squad at White Hart Lane. All the lads were congratulating me and before the game Gazza went over the PA and announced to the crowd, 'We'd all like to congratulate Walshy on the birth of his first son, Alfie!' I've no idea where he got that name from but it was typical of him.

The game was a real 0-0 bore-draw so there was no rocking

baby goal celebration that afternoon, with most of the punters probably half-asleep. At least having Jordan made me re-focus and more determined than ever to make the most of the years I had left in the game. While we slipped down the league, we had at least salvaged the season by reaching the FA Cup final.

Gazza had almost single-handedly taken us to Wembley having scored six goals on the way to the final. He was brilliant on that cup run and was somewhere near his peak. When he was on his game, teams just couldn't handle him.

He scored twice in a 4-2 win over Oxford, twice in a 2-1 win over Portsmouth and got a goal in the quarter-final with Notts County. Then he banged in that brilliant free-kick in the 3-1 semi-final win over Arsenal at Wembley. He was unbelievably good that day considering he had not played for a month following a hernia op.

But on the day of the final against Nottingham Forest a month or so later, I sensed there was something not quite right with him. He was pumped up, charged and full of nervous energy, mainly because I think he wanted to be the star man and show people just how good he really was, but he was just different that day.

When Prince Charles and Lady Diana met the teams before the game, it had to be Gazza who kissed Lady Di's hand for no other reason than he always wanted to be the centre of attention – he was just being himself.

You expected him to do something daft and maybe he was just playing to the gallery because he felt that he had to. We kicked off and he was actually fortunate not to be red-carded about 10 minutes into the game, when he made a ridiculously high challenge on Garry Parker, raking his foot up his chest.

ite Hart gain: I moved to Spurs in 1988. This picture was taken during
natch against Coventry in January 1992

Celebration time: Me and Bev with the FA Cup (above) and celebrating one of two goals against Sunderland in a 3-3 draw in 1990 (left)

Big day: Me on the morning of my wedding at my house in London

Tough opponent: Battling it out v Gary Pallister during a 3-2 win aga Middlesbrough in September 19

up clincher:
le and Gary
labbutt
elebrate the
vn goal from
es Walker
at ultimately
ecided the
991 FA Cup
lal while
elow) I bear
own on Notts
ounty's goal in
e quarter-final
that season's
mpetition

Two headers are better than one: I scored twice for Portsmouth at Old Trafford in a League Cup semi-final first leg match with Manchester United in 1994 – both goals being scored with my hea

Play up Walshy: The away fans at Meadow Lane loved my winner against Notts County in April 1993, but we just missed out on promotion on goal difference

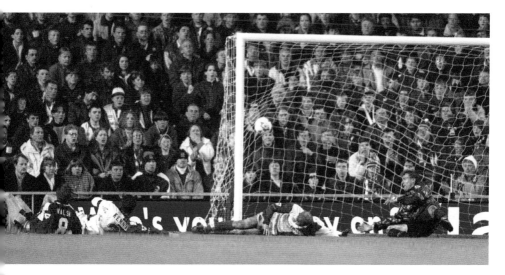

wood score: I scored the deciding goal for Man City in a 3-2 win
t eventual champions Blackburn on a rainy night in April 1995

Blue move: I hit the net twice for City
in a 4-0 win over Everton at the start
of the 1994/95 season. I went on
to play 53 league games for City and
score 16 goals

Second coming: Taking on the West Brom defence during my second stint with Portsmouth in October 1995

Geared up: Me and David Rocastle in Johannesbur, South Africa I got to know Rocky at Mar City – he was a great lad and I wanted picture of hir in my book

Still got it: Back in a Pompey kit for Steve Claridge's benefit match in 2003

arty time: With my old team-mate Gary Mabbutt
uring the 2013 PFA Player of the Year Awards

niley siblings: My two
ns, Jordan and Mason

Straight talker: I've tried to be as honest as I can throughout this book. With me it's a case of what you see is what you get

In my opinion, he'd lost the plot a little because he looked like he wanted to hurt Parker, which was not the Paul Gascoigne I knew. Referee Roger Milford didn't even book him for that challenge, which in turn led to Gazza being the architect of his own downfall. After 17 minutes, he ruptured his cruciate ligaments while making another wild tackle, this time on Forest's Gary Charles.

At first he looked as though he was feigning injury because he knew the ref would punish him this time with Charles still lying on the turf. But Gazza was screaming in pain and it quickly became clear he was badly injured.

It turned out that was the last time he ever played for Spurs, as he would be sidelined for a year and later joined Lazio. Forest scored from the resulting free-kick but Stewie equalised and the game went into extra-time.

I had started as sub but came on after 82 minutes for Vinny Samways with the score at 1-1. I remember thinking I had scored when I got up for a header and saw it looping over Mark Crossley, only for it to strike the bar. From the resulting corner, Des Walker put the ball through his own goal and we won the game 2-1.

The FA Cup was ours and while the hat-trick against Sheffield United was probably was my best moment as a Spurs player, this game had more than made up for missing the cup final at Liverpool. It was something of a rare high for me.

We were all gutted for Gazza and his injury took the shine off the day. Though he would make a comeback of sorts in Italy, he was never quite the same player again. In many ways that was the turning point in his life, which went slowly but steadily downhill thereafter.

WALSHY

My stats for the 1990/91 season were 20 starts with a further 19 appearances off the bench, which meant I had been involved in some capacity in most of the games we played that campaign. I was only just over halfway through my contract with Spurs and something had to change, but I wasn't sure it ever would. I was drifting along and so was my career.

At the start of the 1991/92 campaign, I picked up a groin injury in pre-season and I was a couple of weeks behind everyone else by the time the season began.

I returned for a reserve game against Charlton Athletic where I'd started out and was in reasonably good spirits. I needed a few matches under my belt and felt fine to play the full 90 minutes.

I was working up a decent sweat when I saw we were making a substitution. To be honest, I didn't even look across because I was the senior player in the team. I was playing to get my fitness back up to speed so I could be available for the first team.

So you can imagine my disbelief – and embarrassment – when Ray Clemence, our reserve team manager, decided to haul me off. I didn't get it. I shrugged my shoulders.

Walking over towards him I asked, 'Clem, what's going on? There's still 30 minutes to go.' He stuck out his chest and his demeanour changed to more aggressive. He said, 'Just fucking get off.'

With that, my head went. I trotted over and as I reached the touchline I took my shirt off and threw it in his face, telling him to fuck off for good measure.

As I walked away he threw the shirt back at me, hitting the back of my head. I span around like the Tasmanian Devil and just smacked him right in the bugle in front of the Main Stand, which had around 3,000 people in it.

Next thing, Charlton's Keith Peacock jumped on my back and Clemence had my hands as I was trying to hit him. It must have looked comical for the punters watching this all unfold. It only lasted a few seconds before I traipsed off down the tunnel. I got showered and changed, all the while thinking, 'What the fuck have I done now?'

It was a lovely sunny afternoon in South London and my mum and dad were round at my house. When I got home my mum said, 'Oh hello, love, how did you get on?' I replied, 'Not great, Mum!'

It is funny looking back but it was the end of my time with Spurs, even if I wasn't going to be shipped out immediately. On the Monday morning, there was a picture in the paper of Clemence with a black eye, accompanied by a story saying that Spurs were going to sack me over it.

However, the PFA stepped in and calmed things down. I was suspended for two weeks and had to train on my own. The club thought more time was needed for the dust to settle so I was loaned out to QPR for a month.

Gerry Francis was the manager at the time and I quite enjoyed being at Loftus Road for a few weeks. It would have made sense to make the move permanent because we wouldn't have had to move, which was good from the wife's point of view.

They had Ian Holloway, Alan McDonald, David Bardsley, Ray Wilkins, Garry Thompson, Simon Barker and Gary Waddock among their squad – they were a good group of lads.

I think Gerry Francis would have kept me but he later told me he was quoted £800,000 to buy me, even though I was actually sold for half that amount at the end of the season.

QPR couldn't afford that sort of money and I only played a

couple of games before returning to Spurs, having served my sentence. The first time I played after the bust-up was when I came on as a sub against Manchester City at White Hart Lane and I was given a very warm reception by our fans – presumably not for punching Clem. I still have no idea exactly why I got a reception like that but it made me feel better – I'm not sure how Ray felt.

I still regret hitting Ray that day and, though I've done it in person, I'd still like to acknowledge what I did was wrong and apologise to Ray in print.

There was another moment of madness, too. I recall us playing Norwich and I was on the bench. Yet again, I wasn't in the best of moods after not getting on. Vinny Samways joined me after the game for a quick few laps around the pitch.

We started to jog around the emptying stadium when I heard, 'Your missus is a slag!' from somewhere in the stand. I brushed it off and as we came around for a second lap, I told a steward and said the guy needed moving on. But as we passed the same spot, the same shout came out.

I started running faster and by the time I came around for the third lap, I almost wanted him to say it again and, sure enough, he did. 'Your missus is a slag!'

So I got to where he was and jumped over the wall and into the stand. As I ran up, I realised there were actually two of them. As I got closer, they were getting bigger and bigger and there was just little old me, all on my own.

I couldn't back down now so I lumped one of them in the face then they tried kicking the shit out of me, until the stewards arrived and pulled us apart. I returned to the running and Vinny Samways was pissing himself laughing. When we finished, I had to go and tell Venables there had been 'an incident'. I thought, 'Christ, here we go again' but I wasn't prepared to accept punishment this time. I told the police what had happened and I was relieved that they believed me and agreed there had been provocation.

The two guys ended up getting lifetime bans whereas today, it would be an absolute scandal and they'd throw the book at me – just proves they had more sense back then! You have to be perfect and whiter than white these days, but I don't regret what I did.

I finished the 1991/92 season having played 22 times with a further 15 off the bench, but again, my return of three goals was poor. I still had a year left on my contract and I had to face the fact that I was not far off being 30 and needed at least one more big move to give my family security.

I wasn't sure what lay ahead and though I knew I had a good few years left in me, I didn't realise I had some of the most enjoyable years of my career still to come as I found a couple of managers who believed in me.

15

Any Old Port in a Storm...

I'd had four years at Liverpool and four years at Tottenham, so eight years of my career had been spent with two of the country's biggest clubs, even if things hadn't gone the way I'd hoped at either of them. I still felt I had a lot to give and a move away from Spurs was just what I needed, though it's fair to say that I never envisaged moving out of the top division.

Portsmouth weren't even on my radar when I mulled over where my next destination might be, but at the end of the 1991/92 season, I was informed that they were interested in signing me.

There was a slight complication for me because my agent Eric

Hall was pretty tight with Terry Venables and that relationship may have muddied the waters somewhat.

My first reaction when Eric told me was, 'Fuck off, Eric I'm not signing for them.' They were in what is now the equivalent of the Championship and though they'd just reached the semi-final of the FA Cup and should have beaten Liverpool, I just didn't fancy it.

It was a smaller club, outside the top division and it meant we'd probably have to move again, which wouldn't go down well with Bev. I asked Eric whether QPR were in the mix or not, having enjoyed my brief spell on loan there. He said he didn't think they had the money.

This is where Eric's relationship with Venables complicates matters. Portsmouth's chairman was former QPR chairman Jim Gregory and, as there was nothing else on the table, I went to meet him with Eric and we sat down and talked – out of courtesy more than anything else.

What harm could it do? Sometimes having talks with an interested party begins a chain of events – if there are other clubs interested. So we met and had a chat and because they really wanted me, I knew I had a strong hand.

The mortgage interest rate on my house in London was a massive 16% at the time, so I was insisting on all sorts of things if I signed. I wasn't that interested in the move and I had nothing to lose. They had tabled a four-year contract offer plus agreed a fee of £400,000 with Spurs, but I thought I'd push it as far as I could because ultimately, I was happy to walk away from the deal.

I went to meet Jim Gregory and Jim Smith with Eric and told them the only way I would even think about signing was if they bought my house off me. I knew if they were serious, they'd consider it whereas if they were just sounding me out, it would cool their interest.

The contract offer would take me towards the end of my career and Jim Gregory said they were willing to consider the house purchase. He had also factored in that there would probably be no sell-on value by the time I'd seen out the four years as I'd be 34 by then and probably past my expiry date.

I was surprised when they came back to me and told me they would buy my house and I was also surprised at the amount of money they were offering me, considering they were a Championship side.

The contract was better than the one I'd been on at Spurs, so although I wasn't over-enamoured with the prospect of playing outside the top flight, I agreed to become a Portsmouth player and signed on the dotted line.

In effect, Pompey had called my bluff – I'd got everything I'd asked for, even though I'd thought the negotiations would break down at some point due to my list of demands.

I went along with it because it offered my family the security we needed at that point in our lives. Through your twenties you think your career is going to last forever, but once you edge towards thirty, the end suddenly seems just around the corner.

My first choice would have been QPR as I'd enjoyed my brief spell there, I liked Gerry Francis and it would have meant we could have stayed where we were in London, but it just wasn't going to happen.

There weren't too many clubs that would be a step up after playing for Liverpool and Spurs but I just felt I could have done better. The bottom line was that, despite financially being better off and also being free of a mortgage that had been spiralling out of control, I still didn't want to play for Portsmouth.

The way the whole move had been fast-tracked concerned me. It had happened very quickly, but that was the way it was back then – players were kept in the dark about what was going on. It happened immediately after the season had ended and I felt it was odd that there had been no other interest or even a tentative enquiry.

I'm convinced that if Gerry Francis had been quoted £400,000, he'd have bought me without question and I'd also have signed without question. It wasn't long after I'd penned the contract that I bumped into Gerry and he told me the price he'd been quoted after my loan spell was £800,000 – yet I'd moved to Pompey for half of that. I thought it was a little strange to say the least.

Bev and I went on a family holiday with my mum and dad, my wife's mum and dad and her sister, who was going out with Spurs keeper Ian Walker at that stage. We went to St Lucia for a nice break in the summer sunshine and it gave me chance to take stock of everything.

I pondered the move a lot but the overriding thought in my head was – not for the first time in my life – 'What the fuck have I done?'

I was underwhelmed by the whole affair, but the fact was I'd signed and now I had to somehow get my head around it. I spent a lot of time thinking and working out in the gym during that holiday because, if nothing else, I wanted to arrive at Fratton Park in tip-top condition.

Portsmouth manager Jim Smith was someone I warmed to very quickly – I didn't know him that well before I signed but he is a proper football man, down to earth and easy to get on with. The drive to prove people wrong that I'd had throughout my career, particularly my early days, started to return. If I didn't start well, I was sure the fans would think I'd come for an easy life – a Big Time Charlie on huge wages who couldn't give a fuck.

By the time I arrived for pre-season, the move had begun to grow on me and it felt like I'd got my mojo back again.

For the previous 18 months or so I'd got my act together again, behaving like a proper professional footballer. I was a husband, a father who was eating better, training properly and had got myself back to where I wanted to be for probably the first time in almost three years.

I'd realised I needed to face up to my responsibilities the day Jordan arrived – his birth made me focus all my energies on making the most of whatever playing time I had left.

Portsmouth were getting more than perhaps they realised in that respect. I trained hard throughout the summer and was feeling really good and sharp again, better than I had felt in a long while.

I had no idea what to expect at Portsmouth but what I hadn't been quite prepared for was the culture shock of arriving at an empty Fratton Park and seeing the ageing building and stands – all of which I found a bit depressing.

The training ground facilities at Purbrook were crap, the dressing room and showers were tatty and old and it was a bit deflating. As you'd expect, Liverpool and Tottenham were miles ahead in that respect and had invested a lot more money, but I just expected better.

The training pitches were bumpy and had a slope, and if you

didn't get into the showers early the water was freezing, but there was no point bitching about it – I had to get on with it.

I turned up on day one of pre-season having worked hard all summer and felt fit as a fiddle. I was right up there in all the running sessions and I think, quietly, as the training gradually stepped up, I impressed some of the other players who might have thought I'd be coming to the club to wind down.

My first game was a pre-season friendly away to Dorchester and I remember we played with a Mitre ball, which had a sticky, matt surface to it. When you played on really dry grass, it would get stuck under your foot.

The amount of times I trod on the ball was ridiculous and I was pretty shit in truth. Even though it was only a game to start building our match fitness up, I still went home pretty disappointed because I'd wanted to start well and get off on the right foot in front of the Pompey fans, who'd taken the trouble to come along and watch.

Things gradually improved as we went along and we rounded off pre-season with a win over Tottenham at Fratton Park.

The friendly had been agreed as part of the deal that took me to Pompey and Darren Anderton to White Hart Lane. It was a bit weird to be up against my former Spurs team-mates so soon and I was lucky I saw Neil Ruddock sliding in towards me in one challenge where he tried to come right through me.

We were pretty good mates at Spurs but you'd have never of guessed it from that challenge. I was wondering what the fuck that was all about, but just put it down to his competitive edge once he went on the pitch.

It was a decent home debut for me in front of a good crowd. I won and converted a penalty in a 4-2 win. I was relatively confident that we'd have a good start to the season but all my optimism was about to crash and burn as, for no obvious reason, I started to feel physically sluggish, jaded and lacking energy.

I had no idea why and thought it was a virus of some sort and that I'd shake it off, so I cracked on regardless.

We drew our first game of the season 3-3 against Bristol City, with Guy Whittingham scoring a hat-trick for us. I remember Andy Cole scored a goal for City on his debut having signed from Arsenal. It was the first time I'd clapped eyes on Cole, who I could see straight away was destined for bigger and better things. However, it was Guy who looked as though he was going to be the real star that campaign.

He was a natural goalscorer, which seemed positive for the months ahead. In contrast, I was far from my best and just plodded through the game. There was no obvious explanation because I'd been bombing it in pre-season.

It was the same for the next few games where I was well below par and though we beat Barnsley 1-0, we lost at Leicester and then 4-1 at Brentford so already there was a bit of pressure on us and, I felt, me in particular.

Thankfully, I scored my first goal as we beat Birmingham City 4-0 in the next game, running through the middle before dinking the ball over the keeper, similar to one I'd scored at St Andrews in my Luton Town days.

It was a bit of a relief to get on the scoresheet but I still felt knackered afterwards. I went back to the dressing room and just flopped on the bench and said, 'I feel absolutely fucked.'

Jim Smith just tried to laugh it off and said, 'That's because you're an old fucker, now Walshy.' He was mucking about and trying to have a laugh but I knew whatever the problem was, it wasn't down to age – not unless my body had aged another 20 years overnight.

A week later, it got to the stage where I couldn't even get out of bed because I had no energy. I stayed there for a couple of weeks, sleeping and sweating whatever it was I'd picked up – maybe in St Lucia – out of my body.

The doctor came out to see me a couple of times and said I'd picked up a nasty virus of some kind and that rest was the only cure. It was a month before I was ready to start training again so it hadn't been the ideal start for me.

I feared the fans would already be thinking, 'Useless washed-up twat – why did we sign him?'

Through no fault of my own, I was creating the exact sort of impression I'd worked so hard to avoid.

In effect, I was starting from scratch again, but I still wasn't right. I got back into the training, but the virus had taken everything out of me. I was back in the team to play West Ham but I was poor again and still felt like shit.

I started to wonder whether I'd ever feel like I used to again or whether all the years of living the wrong life had actually caught up with me.

But then, in our next game away to Wolves, I came on as a sub and with one of my first leaps for the ball, I went up for a header and sprang above this big defender.

In an instant, I knew I was back and the virus had finally run its course. The bounce and energy in my legs had returned and from there, I went from strength to strength. My performances got back to where they ought to have been and, better still, I soon struck up a great partnership with Guy Whittingham.

In December 1992, we played Charlton away in what was

my old club's first game back at The Valley after several years of ground-sharing. We headed home with the name Walsh the only scorer – but it was Colin Walsh who notched, not me, and we lost 1-0. It was our only defeat during in an 11-game run that had seen us up to fourth in the table.

The goals were flowing, I was back to peak fitness and I felt like I had a completely new lease of life. After a tricky start to my time on the south coast, I was having a really enjoyable season. I was loving every minute of it and better still, so were the supporters, who loved the style of play and energy we had.

Jim had put together a great team on a shoestring budget that had the right amount of youth and experience and was perfectly balanced. Among others we had Warren Neill, Ray Daniel, Martin Kuhl (who would join Derby a few weeks into the new campaign), a young Kit Symons, Guy Butters and future Pompey boss Andy Awford.

We were probably one of the surprise packages of the division that year and I was more than satisfied with my contribution, although I would have liked to have scored more goals.

We worked really well together as a team. On the wing, we had Mark Chamberlain, a great winger who would later become a father to Alex-Oxlade Chamberlain.

On the pitch, we all knew how to get the best out of each other. I would come short, Guy would go long and Alan McLoughlin would make these great late runs into the box, sprinting past everyone from out of nowhere.

Teams just couldn't handle us because between the four of us, we had so many different, fluid and effective combinations, often with me lying deeper. It would invariably end with the ball being played to Guy, who just didn't miss in that first season.

Meanwhile, off the pitch I was thinking ahead by this point and dabbled in one or two ideas that had been put to me, one of which involved regenerating the club shop. I'd gone in and had a chat with the guy who worked there and was surprised to see how threadbare it was.

A local artist had done a caricature of me so I bought it off him and asked the guy how many T-shirts with a print of my caricature he thought he'd be able to sell.

He said maybe 2,000, so a business associate of mine sourced a manufacturer in Pakistan and shipped them in, making a small profit in the process. The club gave me permission to use the badge and label the gear as official merchandise so I then ordered balls, sports bags and various other paraphernalia and sold them on as well.

The shop was a bit shabby and behind the times and the guy clearly wasn't overly motivated, so I think he appreciated an injection of enthusiasm. They were hardly major business deals I was setting up and there was never going to be a path forward in merchandising for me. It was a bit of fun and nothing more.

Going into our final few games, we had a great chance of winning automatic promotion. We went to Notts County with four games left and I'll never forget running out at Meadow Lane and seeing one end behind the goal packed with Pompey fans – we must have had 6,000 or more there. It was an incredible show of support.

I managed to get the header that won the game 1-0 to make sure we stayed in second place and a week later, we moved to the top of the table with a 2-0 win over Wolves. Chambo set me up for what proved to be a 10th goal of the season as we recorded a 10th victory in 11 games.

ANY OLD PORT IN A STORM...

At that point, with two games to go and two fixtures left against teams we knew we should beat, we looked nailed on to go up. We were one point clear of Kevin Keegan's Newcastle United – who had two games in hand – but three clear of West Ham in third and we had scored one more goal than they had at that point. It was most goals scored, not the goal difference, that counted that season.

Our penultimate game was away to Sunderland at Roker Park and we went there knowing a win would mean we'd need just one more point in the final match at Fratton Park to go up. We had fantastic travelling support again that day but Sunderland were still desperate for points, sitting just two points above second-bottom Birmingham City.

But what should have been a controlled, polished performance by us turned out to be an unmitigated disaster as we somehow completely fluffed our lines. We ended the game with nine men and everything possible going wrong for us.

It started when Guy Butters handled a Sunderland shot with our keeper Alan Knight stranded. The ref had no option but to show him a straight red card. As he walked down the tunnel, Don Goodman rammed home the spot-kick to put Sunderland 1-0 up.

Goodman scored another after the break and we then conceded another to go 3-0 down as our promotion hopes began to collapse. We couldn't just throw in the towel though and I tried to spark us into life. I skipped past two challenges before being tripped in the box.

I couldn't believe the ref didn't give us a penalty and I let him know as much, too. If we had any chance of salvaging anything, we had to get that penalty and score it but the ref

wasn't interested. To say I was pissed off was an understate-
ment and I got a yellow card for my protests – but it was about
to get worse.

The linesman flagged as I walked away because he'd seen
something during the arguing – probably me brushing someone
aside. It was no more than handbags and certainly nothing
malicious but I was shown a red card.

I think I'd accidently caught one of the Sunderland players in
the face with a shrugging-off action but it didn't matter – I was
off and we were down to nine men.

I was livid and as I walked down the tunnel, there was a bag
on the floor so I just booted it as hard as I could – only to find
it was full of spare studs. I was lucky not to break my foot. I got
to the dressing room, smashed all the mirrors and kicked all the
doors in and pretty much wrecked the place.

I was raging and it wasn't long before the police came in and
I knew I was in a bit of bother, not that I really cared at that
stage. None of us could figure out how or why things had gone
so badly. That 4-1 defeat meant we'd gone from favourites to
go up to praying West Ham dropped points in their game the
following day.

I watched West Ham play Swindon Town in the pub. Swindon
had a couple of really good chances with the score at 0-0 but
didn't take them and West Ham went on to win 3-1, which
meant they now had one more goal than us and went into
second spot.

We were at home to Grimsby Town on the last day and West
Ham were home to second-bottom Cambridge United. The
scenario was that so long as we matched West Ham's result, we
just needed to score two more goals than them to go up.

ANY OLD PORT IN A STORM...

On paper, we had much the tougher game because Grimsby were just out of the play-off positions and were a more than useful side, while Cambridge would be relegated if they lost at Upton Park. It was a tense game and we went behind but came back to lead 2-1 – but it wasn't enough – we had more chances to score more but West Ham won 2-0, meaning we finished third and missed out by just one goal.

The Sunderland result had done us irreparable damage and on another day, I think we'd have got a draw or at least scored a few goals. But we'll never know.

Though we were nine points clear of fourth-placed Tranmere, 12 clear of fifth-placed Swindon Town and Leicester City in sixth, we'd ended up in the play-offs. Guy Butters and I were both suspended as we served a three-match bans.

With Filbert Street undergoing construction work, the first leg was played at the City Ground and we lost 1-0 before drawing 2-2 at Fratton Park, so we didn't even make the play-off final. Swindon eventually went up. We'd given it everything but still come up short and our day of madness at Roker Park had cost us dear.

Looking back, the highlight for me had been the football, energy and verve we'd played with.

Whittingham had scored a ridiculous amount of goals – 47 in all competitions and deserved all the plaudits that came his way – though in turned out the Pompey fans reckoned somebody else had actually had a better season than him.

As disappointed as I was, I think if we had gone up, we'd have been the whipping boys of the Premier League because the money wasn't like it is today. I don't think our board would have been able to invest in the squad and get the reinforcements we'd have needed to survive. We'd have just got battered every week and, though I wanted to be back in the top flight, I'm not sure I wanted to be there with Pompey getting turned over every game.

It had been such a fantastic season, one of the most exciting of my career and I was ready for more of the same. I was good to go again, feeling fit and looking forward to another push for promotion.

16

City Slicker

The player that Pompey fans felt had done better than Guy
Whittingham turned out to be me and, unbelievably from my
point of view, I was voted Portsmouth's Player of the Year for
the 1992/93 season, despite Guy breaking every club scoring
record going. It was nice that the fans thought so highly of me,
but I did feel for Guy because how many players score 47 goals
in a season and don't win the player of the year award? I'd more
than played my part, even if I hadn't grabbed all the headlines,
but still, 47 goals – that takes some doing.

Guy must have wondered what he had to do to please the fans
and maybe resigned himself to the fact that if he didn't win
their appreciation then, maybe he never would. I think he may
have got the hump with me a bit because of that, and there

may even be a little bit of resentment towards me to this day, but it was hardly my doing.

Ultimately, it didn't matter because everything was about to change. I returned for pre-season and we headed off for Finland for a few games and a training camp, but there were strong rumours that Guy would be joining Ron Atkinson's Aston Villa for decent money.

Looking at it from Guy's point of view, his stock would probably never be higher and for him, it was now or never.

From my point of view though, it was all a bit deflating because I still wanted to go places and win things but I knew Portsmouth would sell anybody they thought they could cash in on. They wouldn't be trying for one more season to see if we could go up with the players we had.

I was disappointed that they were prepared to break the team up and thought with some of our better players gone, we'd have to start again. I wasn't sure I wanted to be part of that.

I was eager to make up for the lost years and keen to kick on again so I felt pissed off. I couldn't help feeling as though as I was treading water and that we'd never really get anywhere.

Jim Smith looked at replacing Guy, first with Brett Angell, who came to the club for talks but then disappeared. He eventually turned to 33-year-old Lee Chapman, who had been set for West Ham but signed for us instead.

We played alongside each other a couple of times but I found him difficult to play with as I never knew what he was going to do – I couldn't read his game. Within a few weeks, he was off to West Ham, which was probably best for all parties.

Jim then signed Gerry Creaney from Celtic, a stocky striker who had scored a lot of goals in the Scottish Premier League, but he was always going to struggle to fill Guy's boots. In fairness, anyone would have struggled in terms of goals.

Things weren't the same in my second season at Pompey. The simple and effective style of play we'd had with me, McLoughlin and Chamberlain setting up goals for Whittingham was over and we just weren't the same team anymore.

I felt we could still put together a promotion bid but I was already wondering whether I'd ever play in the top flight again – and whether I wanted to stay and find out.

We started with two defeats and lost 5-1 to Crystal Palace in our fifth game as we began with a hangover from the play-off semi-final defeat to Leicester. The goals weren't going in and we'd won just two of our opening 11 matches. We'd slipped to 13th before a run of six wins in eight matches put us back in contention for the play-offs.

We were going well in the League Cup as well, reaching the last eight with a trip to Manchester United to come. So while the verve and adrenaline of my first season wasn't really there, we were doing okay.

We travelled to Old Trafford in early January expecting to be turned over because the power and players they had in their squad was frightening at the time – Eric Cantona, Ryan Giggs, Steve Bruce and Peter Schmeichel to name just a few. But it felt good to be playing back on the big stage and my performance that night effectively put me in the shop window again.

Our league form had dipped badly but we played well above ourselves and were actually unlucky not to win. I scored both our goals in a 2-2 draw and was voted man of the match. Though I felt I'd just played my normal game, I was probably lifted by playing top-quality opposition again

WALSHY

Unbeknown to me, my old Luton Town captain Brian Horton, at that time manager of Manchester City, was in the stands watching that night and I think it's fair to say that was when he made his mind up to try to sign me.

A couple of days later, he called me and asked whether I would be interested in signing for City. The thought of playing in the top division again excited me, especially as I felt I was playing as well as at any time in my career, so I told him I'd definitely be up for the move.

City hadn't challenged for major honours for a long time, but they were still a massive club, regularly pulling in 30,000-plus at Maine Road.

It then became a waiting game as I turned up for training each day expecting to be pulled to one side by Jim and told City were interested. I'd had a fantastic time at Portsmouth but had itchy feet and was disappointed by our transfer policy – it felt like we'd always be a selling club and I could never see a time when that wouldn't be the case.

The partnership with Creaney wasn't anywhere near as effective as the one I'd had with Guy Whittingham so if City wanted me, I was up for it.

It seemed to take an eternity and each day I'd glance at Jim and think, 'What's taking so long?' It went on for a couple of weeks and I began to think it might never happen, but then as I was driving back from training one day, I received the call from Jim I'd been waiting for.

He said Portsmouth had accepted an offer of £750,000 and did I want to go? I did, but a few alarm bells started ringing so I said, 'Yeah, I do – but I think I need to come and see you.'

I could see a stumbling block already and knew there would be a difference of opinion – not with Jim, but with the chairman concerning a discussion we'd had when I first joined the club.

I said to Jim, 'Remember that conversation we had when I first arrived about me having no re-sale value? Well you've had a good 18 months out of me, I'm 32 and you're doubling your money so if I'm leaving, I want some of it,' which I though was fair enough.

Jim told me he didn't have a problem with that but he thought the chairman might have an issue. Jim Gregory had moved on and his son Martin had taken over. While I thought his dad might have been okay with everything, his son would probably see things differently and maybe tell me that agreement had been with his father, not him.

I had a fairly simplistic view on it – if he accepted the money and did the right thing, everyone was a winner, but if he refused to budge, he'd lose the transfer fee and he'd also lose the player he'd had as well. My heart just wouldn't be in it anymore.

I'd done well for Portsmouth and while some people portray footballers as wanting it both ways, sometimes clubs can be the same.

Part of the negotiations had been that this would be my final contract and that the money they were spending would effectively be a write-off but now they were doubling their money and wanting to keep it all for themselves.

I had to be quite hard-nosed about everything and put my point across fairly bluntly. In the end, they agreed to pay me some of the incoming transfer fee and I eventually moved on.

Football can be a dog-eat-dog business and at times, you have to stand up for yourself and fight your corner. I'd never had a problem with doing that throughout my career and had he refused my ultimatum, in all honesty I'd have told him to go and fuck himself.

There was one final twist, though. As I drove up the M6 towards Manchester, West Ham manager Billy Bonds called me and said he also wanted to sign me. He asked me what sort of figures City were talking about and I told him the money I'd been quoted. But I don't think West Ham could match it and that was pretty much the end of it.

It was a pity in some ways because I came from a West Ham family and my dad would have loved to have seen me play for the club he'd supported all his life. Apart from my boyhood side Arsenal, I'd always secretly wanted to play for West Ham – but it wasn't to be.

There was another thought in my head as well – I'd always enjoyed playing at Upton Park but I'd never had a good game at Maine Road. Even when Luton had won there back in 1983, I hadn't played particularly well, so I wondered what was in store for me at City.

It's the old horses for courses theory that you just feel more comfortable and play better at certain grounds but I'd never done well at City.

When I arrived in Manchester, it was dull, miserable, overcast and damp. The streets around Maine Road were all terraced and Moss Side wasn't the most picturesque area I'd ever visited. I found it all pretty depressing.

I went and met chairman Francis Lee, Brian Horton and club secretary Bernard Halford. Then, while I was waiting in another room, I called Eric Hall to find out what West Ham would go to because I still thought the deal could be resurrected.

The thought of playing for the Hammers really excited me

but there wasn't really enough time and I didn't want to put this move in jeopardy, so I signed on the dotted line and I got my head around it all.

Later that day I attended a press conference and I think the media and the fans were probably a bit surprised City were signing a 32-year-old from the second tier.

I think they'd been linked with Dean Saunders and Ian Rush who I'm sure they would have preferred – at least, that's how I was thinking at the time – but they'd got me instead.

I'd always felt I shouldn't have been outside of the top flight. I'd already played 18 months down there which, for me, was long enough. You only get one career and I was nearing the end of mine, so if I could out on a high, so much the better.

Once you've gone down a level, it's natural for people to assume it's because you can no longer cut it at the top, so I think there was an air of scepticism about my signing. I already felt I had something to prove and I had all the motivation I needed.

One of the first lads Brian introduced me to was Uwe Rosler, who had only recently joined City too. Horton was keen to bolster his striking options because Niall Quinn was out with a serious knee injury. With the team managing only 26 goals in 31 games, City were fourth from bottom with just 11 games left.

There was another German lad on trial as well called Steffen Karl and the three of us had a brief afternoon training session at Platt Lane, probably so we could get to know each other a bit better as much as anything else.

We all had to get right in the thick of it as quickly as possible, but there was a nervous tension in the air, the sort you only get when you are moving clubs, because it's a big thing in any player's life. We all just wanted to do well. My son Jordan was around three by this point and my wife had only just started to really settle in the Portsmouth area, so moving north was a big ask. All these things were spinning around my head.

Relegation was still a strong possibility at City and the March transfer deadline had been their last chance of jump-starting the season. Uwe Rosler was something of an unknown quantity and had signed from Bundesliga side FC Nurnberg. There was the added problem that he didn't speak any English – and my German wasn't up to much.

Uwe had played the week before in a 1-1 draw at QPR but we were unveiled as the new strike partnership at home against Wimbledon.

It turned out to be a disappointing start as we went down 1-0 at Maine Road. Wimbledon were a tough, physical side who loved a scrap and enjoyed getting one over on bigger clubs.

It was a hard, scrappy match that didn't go well for either Uwe or me, though we weren't alone as we had precious little service. The pitch was boggy and there hadn't been a hint of understanding between us, though I suppose that was only to be expected.

The problem was we didn't have any time to bed in as the games were running out and we needed to find our feet quickly. We'd now slipped into the bottom three and had just ten games to find enough points to stay up. There was going to be no honeymoon period for anyone, least of all me, who people already had doubts about.

It didn't get any better, either. We were at home again a week later against Sheffield United, another gritty, physical side who liked to play the long-ball game. They were below us in the table and just as desperate for points – and it showed. It was another scrappy, horrible match for the punters and we failed to score again in what was a dour 0-0.

Uwe and I had made no impact whatsoever and initially, things didn't look good. I was trying to work out his game and he was trying to work out mine and it was tough because there was pressure for us to deliver the goods straight away.

I remember after the Sheffield United game, two friends, John and Jill, were driving Bev and Jordan and me back to Portsmouth to sort one or two things out back at the house.

I hadn't stopped in the players' lounge after the game so we pulled into the Sandbach Services on the M6 to get something to eat. I was about third in the queue and feeling a bit fed up with everything when about five or six coachloads of Man United fans poured in – obviously going back to London – and they soon spotted me in the line.

I had a glance around and they were all staring at me. Then it started. They all started singing, 'What a difference you have made! What a difference you have made!' and pointing at me.

It seemed to go on for ages while I waited for my food, then scurried back to my car and set off with the raging hump! Though I didn't appreciate it at the time, in hindsight, it was pretty funny.

Things did start to improve and gradually, the pieces began to fall into place. I could see Uwe liked running into the channels and trying to get behind the opposition's back four, whereas I liked to come short and collect the ball from deep. A partnership began to form.

It took four games for us to really get going and the arrival of Peter Beagrie from Everton was maybe the catalyst for the improvement. Beags gave us something different because we now had width on both sides with Nicky Summerbee bombing down the right flank – we started to stretch defences.

We played on the 'beach' at Oldham and drew 0-0. While we weren't exactly pulling up trees, it was another point on the board. Our next match was Ipswich Town away and we drew again, this time 2-2, but should have won.

More importantly, both Uwe and I scored and we never really looked back after that. First of all, Beags raced down the left wing, cut inside and hit a shot with his right foot that the Craig Forrest just managed to tip onto the post. The ball came to me and I managed to stretch out a leg out and bundle it over the line for my first goal for City.

It was a massive weight lifted because we'd gone something like five hours without scoring between us. It added a spring to my step and I felt confident again.

When the ball came into me later in the game, I shaped to shoot before sliding in Uwe, who made it 2-1. So we'd both broken our duck in the same game and things really took off.

We should have gone on and won the game but Michel Vonk gave a daft penalty away as he brought down one of their players in the box, despite the fact he'd been running away from goal. We had to settle for yet another draw.

Uwe and I were starting to enjoy playing together though and the goals began to fly in. We won our next three games against Aston Villa, Southampton and Newcastle and ended up losing just one of our last ten, with Uwe and I scoring nine goals between us.

We stayed up comfortably in the end and while I could sense the City fans were warming to me, they loved Uwe. He had done fantastically well given all the obstacles he'd had to overcome and he was a great guy as well, so I was happy for him.

Bev and I decided to initially base ourselves at Mottram Hall Hotel in Mottram St Andrew and settled in immediately and found we made friends really easily.

Your life off the pitch is just as important as the one on it and if the family are happy, usually that will transmits itself into performances. I was already looking forward to my first full campaign as a City player.

17

Mr Sky Blue

It had been an enjoyable first few months with City and I felt really good, both mentally and physically. I did wonder what the Portsmouth fans had made of me leaving as I would imagine they would have thought I'd be there until I hung my boots up. I know that it hadn't gone down too well when I signed for City, but it was the chairman who had got all the flak.

As it happened, I didn't have to wait long to find out. At the end of the 1993/94 season, Alan Knight, Pompey's long-serving goalkeeper, had a testimonial at Fratton Park to mark 16 years with the club – it might have been his second or third testimonial as he'd been there that long – and I was one of three former players invited back to play in the game.

Mark Hateley, Barry Horne, Darren Anderton and several

other guest players turned out and we were introduced on to the pitch individually before kick-off.

It didn't take me long to realise the fans understood why I'd gone and could see the move had been the right thing for me at the stage of my career.

I'd played a part in keeping City in the Premier League and enjoyed one last fling at the top level and it clearly wasn't held against me. The reception I got when I came out was absolutely fantastic and something I'll never forget.

It felt good that I'd done well at City and proved one or two people wrong in the process. I could still run out at Fratton Park and stick my chest out, which filled me with pride.

After a family holiday and some time back down south, I returned to City to begin the pre-season. We flew out to Sweden for a training camp and while we were out there, Uwe met a Norwegian girl called Cecile. They began seeing each other while we were over there – a relationship that would later end in marriage and produce two sons, Tony and Colin – but all that was a long way off at that point.

The air was clean and fresh in Norway and the scenery was fantastic. I remember being in on the team coach during that trip with Brian Horton and David Moss, looking for our hotel. We stopped at crossroads and on one side there was a sign that said 'Horton' and on the other there was a sign saying 'Moss' – it was a really small town in the middle of nowhere. What are the odds?

We had a good pre-season with both Uwe and I feeling part of everything – we were confident of having a decent campaign. Steve McMahon was still at the club and gave us a bit of steel and experience in midfield, we had two great wingers in Beags and Summerbee plus Garry Flitcroft and Steve Lomas were knocking on the door as well. So there was plenty of optimism around the place, but despite the feelgood factor, we started with a 3-0 defeat at Arsenal.

We bounced straight back with successive wins at Maine Road, beating West Ham 3-0 and then hammering Everton 4-0. The latter game saw me score one of my favourite career goals after winning the ball on the edge of our box and then finishing off the move with a sweet shot past Neville Southall (again).

Uwe and I had a formed great understanding and we'd both scored three goals in the first three games. Plus, Niall Quinn had returned from injury and with the crosses we were getting from the flanks, we were as good as any side in the Premier League when we attacked.

Brian Horton would try to accommodate Uwe, Niall and myself up front if we were fit – there were times when we just clicked and blew teams away.

We used to love attacking the North Stand, which was full of the Kippax fans that had been relocated because the old terrace had been demolished to make way for a new stand.

The atmosphere was electric and the noise and singing all came from that end. Though I didn't keep count, it felt like we scored most of our goals in front of the North Stand.

I can honestly say that winning the City fans over is one of the proudest achievements of my career. I'd gone to a club where I believe the fans hadn't really wanted me – something I'd never really experienced before on my travels – but I'd won them over in a relatively short space of time.

As I said previously, it was maybe because they had initially felt I was too old and past my best, plus I was teaming up with a player I didn't know from Adam, yet I'd played a big part in helping keeping us stay in the Premier League. In turn, the City supporters had really taken to me and Uwe.

I was proud of the hurdles we'd both overcome, though when I look back, I can't blame their scepticism. I'd done nothing of any real note at Spurs, then I had dropped out of the top flight for 18 months and gone off radar at Portsmouth – all that, plus I was in my 32nd year, so I understood it all.

The team were flying and we were as high as sixth in the table by early December, just six points behind third placed Newcastle United with only leaders Blackburn Rovers having scored more home goals than we had. Maurizio Gaudino arrived on loan while Steve McMahon left to become player-manager of Swindon Town.

There were some real characters at the club at that time – not quite the fruit and nut selection we'd had at Spurs – but nonetheless, when you've got somebody like John Burridge in your squad, life is never dull.

I remember when we are all having lunch one day and he asked us all to throw bread rolls at him to test his reflexes – it was an invitation too good to miss. We all started pelting him with them and a few caught him plum in the face.

He was a great lad but an absolute nutter. At home, he used to ask his wife to throw a ball that he kept in the lounge at him randomly when he wasn't expecting it – eating his dinner or watching TV – so he could catch it and keep his reflexes sharp.

He was hilarious and had an infectious personality that was great to be around. He was a top pro too, and loved his training. He was always working hard and staying behind for extra sessions. Like most keepers, the thing he hated most was being chipped and I got him one day with a beauty that he could only watch deftly sail over his head and into the net. I could see he was fuming.

I'd wind him up, saying, 'Come on Budgie you should have go that one! Come on mate, up your game!' I loved taking the piss when anything like that happened, just as I had done with a succession of keepers before him.

There was another occasion when we were away to Tottenham and Andy Dibble felt unwell overnight, so Budgie was told he'd be playing. If he did, he would set a new record for being the oldest player to play in the Premier League.

But it had been lashing it down all night and by the time kick-off was near, the pitch was waterlogged and the game was called off.

Budgie, who had been champing at the bit to play, was gutted. We rubbed it in of course, saying, 'Unlucky Budgie, maybe next time.' Thankfully, he did eventually get the record a bit later on that season at the age of 43, so all was not lost.

Our captain at the time was Keith Curle and in all honesty, I don't think he was a particularly good skipper. He was a top player but he had a touch of arrogance and cockiness about him – which I didn't mind – but I don't think he was quite as good as he thought he was.

He wasn't a bad bloke but he was a bit selfish sometimes and wasn't the sort of captain who wanted to get into the role and do things for everyone.

There were times when he'd push everyone up high because he was fast and fancied himself against anyone, whereas Alan Kernaghan, his central defensive partner, wasn't quick and would sometimes get caught on the counter-attack. All in all though, he was a decent lad that I got along well with. Back on the pitch, the 5-2 win over Spurs in October had been fantastic and it was extra special because it was against my former club. I was determined to show the Spurs fans the real Paul Walsh that day, not the shadow of a player they'd seen for the best part of four years.

In simple terms, the Spurs fans had never really seen the best of me, so it was them I wanted to impress as I had no grudge against the club. They had spent big since I left and were a quality side with Jurgen Klinsmann, Ilie Dumitrescu, Gheorghe Popescu and Teddy Sheringham among others, so it was a cracking result for us.

I remember watching Match of the Day and hearing John Motson claim it had been one of the best games he'd ever seen. Everything just clicked for us that day and the only disappointment was that I only scored two goals.

I missed the easiest chance of the lot when I headed a cross straight at Ian Walker, with Quinny nodding the rebound in – I should have had a hat-trick that day, but there you go. I know Uwe was gutted because he'd picked up an injury and had wanted to go up against fellow countryman Klinsmann but never had the chance.

I loved every minute of it because at that stage of my career, I never thought I'd have the chance to play regularly in the top flight. I knew it wouldn't last forever so was making the most of it.

By the time I scored twice in a 3-3 draw with Southampton at Maine Road, I'd scored nine goals in 13 Premier League games, which was right up there with the best spells of my career. I was 32 and was still going well but when Quinny returned, I was asked to play left midfield for a time with Beags out injured. As the season went on the results started to turn against us, with no wins in ten between early December and late February, when we found the net just five times.

I hadn't scored for three months in the league but the gaffer continued to play me, perhaps thinking things would eventually turn around for both the team and for me. His faith probably worked against us both because the truth was I needed a break and to be rested at certain points in the season.

I think of the first 60-odd games that were played after I joined City, I featured in 58 of them. I missed two games with injury after a bad tackle by a Man United-supporting local DJ called Mike Sweeney during a friendly against Droylsden when I went right over on my ankle, but that was it.

I'd just needed a breather here and there because my levels dipped occasionally and I was at a stage of my career when my fitness needed to be managed correctly.

The moment that really hit home that age was catching up with me was when we lost 2-1 at home to Arsenal in mid-December and, though I had a decent game, for the first time in my career – the virus at Pompey notwithstanding – my legs didn't respond to a situation.

A cross came in from the left, I went to jump and head the ball but nothing happened and I felt I was jumping with lead weights in my boots. That worried me, and though I initially thought I was just tired and my legs were dead, in reality it was the first signal from my body that things were in decline.

I needed to be fresh to be at my sharpest and that sometimes eluded me in certain games, but because Horton never rested me – which also pleased me on some levels – I wasn't having the recovery time I needed. If I'd been left out of the odd game I'd have been disappointed but I would have understood and benefited from the break.

Part of me needed a rest, but part of me was desperate to make up for lost time and didn't want to miss another game. It was a complex situation to be in.

By the end of December, Uwe and I had scored 22 goals between us, which is a fairly prolific partnership by anyone's standards. We'd scored 23 goals between us in our first eight league games at Maine Road. I was rubbing shoulders right up there with Robbie Fowler, Alan Shearer and Les Ferdinand, but I just couldn't sustain that form and, as a team, we began to falter alarmingly.

One win in 15 Premier League games saw us plummet into 16th, just five points above the relegation places. For whatever reason, we couldn't buy a win and the goals had dried up.

Nobby, as Horton was sometimes known to the lads (or I shortened it to just Nob when he got on my nerves) was under intense pressure as we came towards the end of the 1994/95 season and there were strong rumours in the media that he might be replaced.

We knew a poor run of results wasn't going to help matters but we were in a rut and were looking more like relegation candidates every week.

Overall, I think mid-table would have been a more realistic reflection of the season as a whole and the quality we had shown at times, particularly in the first half of the campaign.

Though we'd slipped down the table and lost much of our zip, there were still one or two high points along the way, one of which was a period of four days when we had a couple of wins that guaranteed we wouldn't be involved in the end of season relegation scrap. We beat Liverpool 2-1 at Maine Road and then we won 3-2 away to soon-to-be-crowned champions Blackburn Rovers, where I also managed to score the winner.

During the game at Ewood Park, I came across an old adversary, Graeme Le Saux, who I always thought was a decent player and had an edge to his game that I'd never had a problem with.

I felt he always liked to leave something in when he went in for a challenge, but it was part of the game and it always made for an interesting 90 minutes when I was up against him.

During this game we were more than holding our own and had won a free-kick on the edge of the Blackburn box, where I positioned myself on the end of the wall with Le Saux next to me.

He made out he was putting his hand up in the air to appeal about something or other and as he did he half-punched me across the face. He left his arm up in the air for a few seconds and when the ref looked away, he brought his arm down and elbowed me in the stomach.

I'd sort of expected he would try something again so I was ready for it and tensed my muscles. The dig didn't bother me, but I was about to bother him.

He was trying to attract the referee's attention to protect himself but I didn't care if the ref was looking or not as I smashed Le Saux as hard as I could in the back of the head. I have to add that I enjoyed every second of it.

I quickly moved away from where I'd been standing, the ref hadn't clocked it and that was the end of the matter.

I never slept particularly well after night games because my mind was invariably racing around, replaying what had happened, so I stayed up to watch the highlights on Sky Sports.

Watching the re-run of my spat, which the cameras had picked up, I got even more pleasure when I saw my punch up close – in plain view of the watching millions – followed by Le Saux running away, rubbing the back of his head in considerable pain.

I still feel that City chairman Franny Lee had already made his mind up that he wanted to replace Horton and, after what was a great win at Ewood Park, I thought he looked almost disappointed we'd won because it meant he couldn't sack him.

I don't know that for a fact and that's just my reading of the situation. It could be that I got the wrong impression, who knows? I'm sure Franny has his own thoughts on that!

Those were the last two wins of the season and we failed to win any of our last four. A 3-2 defeat to QPR on the final day saw us drop to 17th – a win would have seen us finish 12th, which would have looked a lot better on paper. It was deflating to end with such a damp squib.

Overall though, I'd had another good season and the fans were fantastic with me. We'd played entertaining football in the early months of the campaign and scored plenty of goals. Though we badly tailed off after Christmas, I think the City supporters accepted we'd kicked on from the previous year, even if we hadn't fulfilled our early season promise.

It also proved I had been right to leave Pompey when I did. Had I not, I would never have had that last fling in the top flight that I had believed – and had now proved – I was capable of.

One thing City fans love is somebody who never gives in and is always prepared to work hard for the cause. I think that was the key to Uwe and I gelling so well and being accepted.

I remember former manager Tony Book, who was on the coaching staff when I was at Maine Road, telling me to make sure I waved to the Kippax when I ran out because they'd love that – and I always did.

I was full of confidence and I loved living in Manchester, where my wife, Jordan and I were happy. We could have easily stayed in the area permanently because living back in the north-west had been a breath of fresh air, but things were set to change for me and the club. Ultimately, it would not be for the better.

The fact we'd won just four of the last 24 Premier League games meant Brian Horton, who had been on borrowed time since Franny came in, was finally sacked. Going into my third season at City, everything had changed completely.

I was really disappointed for Nobby because I'd known and worked with him on and off for a long time, but it had been inevitable. Though he was popular with the fans, he wasn't a big enough name for City.

He could moan when he wanted to and as a player, he was the biggest moaner I ever came across. I loved it that he'd been my manager and as a former team-mate, that he'd wanted me to play for his club, but he was on his way and there was nothing I could do about it.

I took my first coaching badge at the end of the campaign with former City keeper Alex Williams in charge. My heart wasn't really in it and I was knackered because it was the day after our final game of the season. I just didn't want to be there.

I think Alex almost gave the badge to me and I was surrounded by people who had never really been involved in the game, but I got through the four-day course, thinking it might be of some use one day. Perhaps sooner rather than later given my age at the time. With a new manager to come and an uncertain few months ahead, I had plenty to mull over during the summer.

18

Ball and Chain

I might have been one of the few people who wasn't disappointed when City announced that Alan Ball was to be our next manager, though the ideal situation for me on a personal level would obviously have been to have Horton stay on. Like Horton, Ball wasn't the big name the fans had expected and probably wasn't even on their radar, but he was a friend of Franny Lee and someone he obviously trusted.

Ball was one of my childhood heroes and now I was going to be working under him for the first time, so I was looking forward to seeing how he managed.

Just before the start of the 1995/96 season, he turned up at Platt Lane for training and his first day speech was, for me, rousing and inspirational. I thought he would go on to do well at City. He spoke with passion and the things he said made sense. I liked what he was thinking. Despite this, it didn't take long to discover that, although Alan was portrayed in the media as quite bubbly and bright, I actually found him quite miserable and demotivating.

I could see the new campaign being a massive struggle, sensing things weren't right in pre-season. I could see both the team – and me in particular – were going to struggle with Ball's new system, which put a lot of square pegs in round holes.

Though I had no idea at the time, an unexpected phone call while we were in Edinburgh for a friendly with Hearts turned out to be the start of my move away from City.

It was just a week before the opening game of the campaign and the night before the game against Hearts, I got a call in my hotel room from Terry Fenwick, my old room-mate from my Tottenham days. He had since taken over as the new Portsmouth manager.

He wanted my opinion on two City players he was thinking of signing, Fitzroy Simpson and Carl Griffiths. He knew I wouldn't bullshit him so I said, 'Fitz will do a good job but Griff is a lazy fucker, though he might score you the odd goal if you can get him playing. He's a lazy twat and he'll drive you mad.'

I think he ended up taking both players despite my testimonials (!) and while Fitz worked out well, as predicted, Griff didn't. While Fen was on the phone I tested the water a little by asking, 'Well, don't you want me back as well?'

He sounded interested and said, 'Why, would you come?' I told him I would definitely think about it if the opportunity arose. He asked me to leave it with him and that was the start of it. We lost 5-1 against Hearts and I lasted an hour as I was recovering from a groin strain I'd picked up a week or so before. The whole game, friendly or not, was a demoralising experience and it turned out to be a precursor of things to come.

Ball was quickly becoming obsessed with new signing Georgi Kinkladze and he told the journalists gathered at the eve of season press conference that Georgi 'would have people hanging from the rafters trying to watch him play' – this before anyone had really seen him kick a ball.

The lads used to say that whenever Bally saw Georgi in training he used to have a little dribble in his shorts. Ball wanted to build the team around Georgi and change the whole dynamic of the side, but it was never going to work.

Don't get me wrong, Georgi had amazing individual ability and if you put his top five goals on YouTube, they'd rival any great player on the planet. But Ball indulged him and was prepared to look past the negative aspects of his game, which for me, far outweighed his positives.

The problem as I saw it was that Ball played Kinkladze behind the two strikers, so the two wingers had to tuck inside, meaning they were no longer actually out and out wingers. In turn, we lost our width, with Beags and Summerbee's wings well and truly clipped.

We lost the effectiveness of our wingers who had supplied the lion's share of crosses that Quinny, Uwe and I had scored from, plus everything I brought to the table, all just to accommodate one player.

For all his silky skills and occasional brilliance, he just wasn't worth it. He was supremely talented, but it wasn't enough. In today's game you might be able to get away with Georgi playing behind the striker and potentially relieve him of a bit of defensive responsibility. But because everybody played 4-4-2 back then, Ball's system, which was more like a 4-3-1-2 with Georgi in the hole in what I'd label the 'luxury role', just didn't work.

For my game, it was a disaster because for the first time in 18 years of playing senior football, I didn't know where to run. The opposition full-backs could now tuck in because we had no wingers to mark and it was so congested in the central area with me, Uwe and Georgi almost falling over each other.

It buggered my game up completely and I could see we'd lost our threat to accommodate Georgi – in short, Bally had set us up to fail. I couldn't believe that such a knowledgeable football man couldn't see that everything was wrong and that the whole team was revolving around just one individual.

Georgi didn't contribute enough and we weren't good enough to carry him in the games when he wasn't delivering the goods.

I played in the first three matches of the 1995/96 season and though we drew 1-1 with Spurs in the opening game, the team was about to embark on a nightmare run that would leave the club rooted to the foot of the table.

Things quickly came to a head for me during a 2-1 defeat at Coventry, when I was moving into my usual position behind Uwe. I'd look up to see Georgi stood a few feet away every time. This was happening time and time again and it wasn't going to work. I would play one more game for City and just three games in, I was again on my travels.

Something had to give and at the age I was at, I wanted to enjoy the last few years of my career. I couldn't see the obsession with Georgi ending any time soon so when a rumour surfaced in The Sun suggesting Ball was looking to bring Gerry Creaney in from Portsmouth, I brought things to a head by manipulating the situation. I went to see Ball and I said, 'Look, if you want to bring Creaney in, it's not a problem but don't fuck me about. I've had 18 great months here and I think I've done well for the club. Just don't take the piss out of me. Get the deal done and I'll go.'

I could only see the season being a massive struggle and I was fast approaching my 33rd birthday. So when Ball got a whiff that Terry Fenwick might be interested in taking me back to Portsmouth – a situation I'd not discouraged a few weeks before – I think he sensed he could get a deal that suited all parties, with Gerry Creaney coming in and me moving in the opposite direction.

Kit Symons had signed for us in the summer from Pompey and as soon as he heard rumours I might be leaving, he said, 'Walshy what are you doing to me?' I don't think he was too keen to have Gerry as a team-mate again – but that was not my problem anymore.

A deal was agreed between the two clubs not that long after and I was on my way. I'd had 18 fantastic months with City and my time there was right up with my career highs, but I needed to move on.

Portsmouth made me a great offer and a three-year contract at a club I liked and where I already knew the fans rated me – it made perfect sense. The contract would take me to my 36th birthday and the way I was feeling, that would probably be just about right.

I had to do it for my family and my own security. Without trying to be wise after the event, it turned out to be a sensible move, with City bottom of the league by Christmas.

For me, Georgi had been the catalyst for City's problems. For a player who the whole team operated around, he didn't score enough goals, didn't make enough goals, didn't tackle, didn't head it and his overall contribution wasn't enough – not for the ability he had.

The City fans could see Kinkladze was a talented player and loved it when he turned on the magic, but I saw things differently. The question that I think the City fans never asked was, if you were playing a better team and they had the ball, what was Georgi doing? The answer was fuck all.

Ball thought he was brilliant – but I didn't. I'm sure a lot of City fans will say, 'Leave off Kinky, he was unbelievable' but I'd just remind them what happened to the team that season.

I can't say what might have happened had he never signed in the first place. Ball would have made his own changes and brought in some of his own players – managers always do – but putting your faith blindly in one player is a dangerous thing to do and it probably cost Ball his job further down the line.

The whole experience tarnished my image of Ball a little but he never slagged me off and was always fair with me.

However, for City chairman Franny Lee, my move to Portsmouth was not necessarily a good thing. Whether he'd thought he was being clever when I first arrived or not, I'm not sure but he didn't pay me a signing-on fee, saying I could have 15% of any sell-on fee instead. Maybe he believed – with good reason – I would be finished when I eventually left City on a free.

So when the swap deal was in progress, I called Paul Weld, the club secretary at Portsmouth and somebody I knew quite well. I asked him what I was being valued at in the deal and he told me £800,000 and he had a fax to prove it.

I think the fee was more of a paper exercise and was set that high so City fans wouldn't grumble too much. I thought that was a more than fair price for a 33-year-old who the club had got a good 18 months out of.

So I wasn't quite done and dusted at City. I still had to have the same sort of conversation with Franny as I'd had at Portsmouth with Martin Gregory, who had also agreed figures probably based on the assumption I wouldn't be moving on.

Franny and I had a bit of a stand-off until we agreed that £600,000 was a fair price for my transfer fee to be valued at. This became the basis of my sell-on percentage fee.

I bumped into Franny in 2014 for the first time in a while and he recalls events slightly differently, but this is my book and my version of events.

So I was going back to Fratton Park and there would be no apprehension this time. I knew the fans would accept me back as they'd been sad to see me go the first time and there would be no surprises regarding facilities and suchlike.

I'd never been seen as the bad guy in the move to City and had remained popular so I had nothing to prove to anyone. I wanted to play my part in a team that could hopefully win promotion and help get the club back in the top flight.

I never thought of Portsmouth as a gentle way of ending my career – I never would have done that anywhere.

We knew the area, the house I'd had been having built was almost finished and there was a lot of positives to the move back to the south coast – plus Bev was pregnant with my second son, Mason. This was another reason to move back down south, as we had no family support network in Manchester to help with the kids.

We moved into a hotel while the final jobs on the house were done and Mason arrived on 22 November 1995 at St Mary's Hospital in Portsmouth. Again, it puts everything into perspective when you are holding another beautiful baby in your arms.

Like his brother, he came out of the sun roof rather than a natural birth on the recommendation of the doctors.

I was probably as settled as I had been at any point in my life, both personally and professionally. The Pompey fans had always been good to me and I was looking forward to playing in front of them again.

As I'd joined just after the season had started, I couldn't play straightaway. So there was a massive build-up to my second home debut, which gave me about 10 days to get myself focused and match fit.

For my first game, we were up against Derby, a team strongly fancied to win the Championship and managed by my old boss Jim Smith. It felt great to run out at Fratton Park again. We drew 2-2 and I was loving it all.

I knew I still had plenty to offer, even if my legs maybe weren't quite up to top flight-football anymore. That said, I could have maybe adjusted my game to reduce the all-action, high energy style I'd always played with.

I could have dropped back behind the strikers or into central midfield – there were options and, as time went on, I would've been happy to consider all of them.

There was one moment that sticks in my mind in my second spell at Pompey and that was a goal against Ipswich Town. I picked the ball up on the halfway line and drove forward.

I shaped to hit a powerful shot before sliding a lob wedge under it. Craig Forrest, who was a giant of a goalkeeper, just floundered as the ball sailed over his head. I'd always loved chipping keepers – especially ones that tall – and it was without doubt one of the best goals I had ever scored.

We lost the game in the last minute as Neil Thompson scored a fantastic free-kick – but it wasn't as good as my goal!

I scored home and away against Luton Town but I didn't get as many as I would have liked, though I was more or less on a par with my career average of one goal every three matches.

Paul Hall was chipping in with a few, Alan McLoughlin and Martin Allen were all scoring regularly from midfield and Jimmy Carter was supplying the ammunition from the wing, but this was largely a different side from my first spell. Mark Chamberlain and Guy Whittingham had long since gone.

Though I got on really well with the rest of the lads and felt I had their respect, there was one time in training that ended in a punch-up. Guy Butters was a big six foot four- inch lump of a central defender and during one session at the Royal Navy base in Portsmouth he came in way over the top from behind – far more aggressively that he normally would – and I wondered why he'd done it. I turned around and said, 'You want to try doing that in a fucking game.'

I'd let him know I wasn't happy with the challenge, but a few minutes later the ball came into me again and Butters went right through the back of me again. This time, I really had the hump so I got up and started to lay into him.

Because he was big and cumbersome, his punches weren't getting anywhere near me whereas I landed four or five before the lads pulled us apart. I felt he'd taken cheap shots down my calf in training and I was pleased I'd stood my ground because the size difference meant it was a bit of a gamble.

It was out of character and I still don't know to this day why he did it. He's a good lad and I still get on well with him today but whereas he was bleeding afterwards, I didn't have a mark on me. Whatever the agenda was, we moved on and it didn't happen again. I was 33, enjoyed training and I didn't need it but he'd gone too far that day.

I was playing my part and enjoying my football, even if we had been struggling near the bottom for a while. We improved around Christmas and started to pull away from the drop zone but for me, things were about to come to an abrupt end.

I had no idea that the header I scored against Grimsby Town on 13 January 1996 would be the last goal of my career because when the end came, there was no warning or chance to prepare – it came from nowhere.

You don't forget moments like that and I recall the day and moment vividly. We were away to Millwall and there was no crunching challenge or a career-ending tackle – when it happened, like many of the worst injuries in football, it looked pretty innocuous from the outside.

I miscontrolled a pass and in trying to retrieve it, lunged at the ball with my left leg, which meant my right leg was tucked underneath my body. As my body weight fell down, my backside crunched my heel and I strained my knee.

I felt a sharp pain on the lower right-hand side of the knee so I limped off and was later booked in to see the surgeon. The following day, X-rays showed I had a micro-fracture at the top of my fibula. I was told a day or so later that I should rest it for three weeks and I'd be fine.

Ten days later, Terry Fenwick asked our physio Neil Sillett, 'Do you think Walshy can give it a go on Saturday?'

Having been in the same situation at Liverpool and having

paid dearly for the decision I made, you'd think I would err on the side of caution, but no. Against my better judgement and because I wanted to help Fenners – plus not wanting to seem a soft arse – I said I'd try.

We walked over to Milton Park near to Fratton Park and I had a fitness test – of sorts. I had a little jog around and at the start, I was limping about a bit with some discomfort. As we carried on, it got a bit easier, though it was never exactly comfortable.

Fitness tests aren't ever going to be as strenuous as a real game so they only have so much use, but they are a decent indicator as to where you're at. Or at least that's what you hope.

So, just a fortnight after sustaining the original injury, I was declared fit for the home game against Leicester City. Though I wasn't 100%, I was doing what the manager had asked me.

I gave it a go and things were manageable until about 20 minutes in when the ball went out towards Leicester's left full-back and I sprinted over to close him down. As I planted my right leg down, my knee basically collapsed. The rest of my knee had been compensating for the micro-fracture injury and the whole lot went as a result.

I was strapped up and stretchered off, fearing it was bad but not entirely sure what the extent of the injury was. Later, a number of Pompey fans wrote to me saying they heard a loud pop as my ligaments snapped – as I had – and that was it. I would never play competitively again.

I'd been captain of Portsmouth, leading the team out one minute, never to appear again as a professional footballer the next. It was a surreal feeling but the fact was that, at the age of 33, I was finished.

As my knee was examined, I could tell it was a cruciate

ligament problem, because they were testing for any laxity in the knee and it was moving around a fair bit.

So when I went for the scan, I was already expecting the worst. When it was confirmed I'd ruptured my anterior cruciate ligament, at my age, I knew it would be difficult to come back.

After an exploratory operation I was advised that the state of my knee was such that it would be unwise to play again. The surgeon felt I'd never get back to where I'd been because age and time were both against me.

Despite the advances made 20 years on, I'm not sure whether the prognosis would have been any different today.

I was devastated. I knew my playing days were coming towards an end but like anyone else, I wanted it on my terms. At that point, I still had two-and-a-half years left on my contract and if I had changed positions and relied less on speed and agility, I maybe could have carried on even longer.

I would have certainly given everything a try before hanging my boots up because I still felt I was making up for those lost years. That said, I'm not sure how I'd have felt I knew if I couldn't get past people or influence the game in the way I wanted anymore. It probably would have driven me mad and I'd have called it a day anyway. I'll never know.

I couldn't quite get my head around the reality of what was going on at the time. I'd never play again – something no footballer wants to ever hear.

You want to be in control and decide when your body can't match your desire. You want to decide you've had enough of training, decide you are tired of missing the weekends with your family – not have the decision made for you.

I cried for a few days and I went into a period I can only

describe as mourning as I came to terms with the fact my career was over.

I had so many thoughts rolling around my head – what do I want to do next? What am I going to do with the rest of my life? I was in a dark place and this time I couldn't see any light at the end of the tunnel…

19

The Invisible Man

With 30 months of gainful employment at Portsmouth FC still to serve, I had to work out how I was going to manoeuvre myself around and find a suitable role at the club. It's funny how quickly some people's attitude changes towards you because suddenly, you're no use as a player anymore.

From being the centre of attention and part of the beating heart of the club, you become just part of the furniture and I detected that change in more than a few individuals.

I was still on a decent contract and though I was recovering from a serious injury, I couldn't expect to just run my deal down doing nothing in the time that remained. I was still having exploratory operations and undergoing various procedures as well as rehabilitating my knee slowly. So initially that took up the final months of the 1995/96 season. There is a process where the surgeon looks inside your knee to confirm the prognosis, and then there is a period of time where you try to strengthen the knee before having the major operation to reconstruct the joint.

For the first six months or so, it was all about a rebuilding and damage-limitation process. I didn't know where I stood in the grand plan of everything at Portsmouth, as nothing had been discussed in any great detail and I still hadn't officially retired.

Terry Venables became the club's director of football in July 1996. He was as popular as ever following a successful stint as England manager at Euro '96, but I wasn't convinced.

England's performance at Euro '96 hadn't been as impressive in my eyes as it had been for the rest of the nation. We hadn't had to qualify and there was only one stand-out performance – the 4-1 win over Holland. The rest had been just okay.

There was a draw with Switzerland, a win over Scotland (who missed a penalty), a penalty shoot-out win over Spain (who should have beaten us) and then defeat to Germany in the semis.

I just didn't get wrapped up in the euphoria of it all and I wondered if his arrival would impact on me. As it was though, he was rarely seen about the place due to other commitments, which included managing the Australian national team.

Meanwhile, my business deals indirectly led to me being offered a role in the commercial department – something I didn't really want. Some at the club questioned whether I should be doing this kind of thing in the first place as I was technically still in rehab, but I wanted to stay involved with the football side. People obviously thought I had something to offer commercially, so there were one or two issues still to be resolved.

On the subject of my future, I soon found the saga that unfolds on the back of a career-ending injury is like nothing you've ever prepared for. I suppose the reality was that I needed to do a deal with the club over the insurance policy they had on me so we could all move on.

They still had more than two years of paying me a full wage ahead of them and it made sense for all parties to agree a way forward. The outcome of the amicable discussions with chairman Martin Gregory and chief executive David Deacon was that I accepted a role on the backroom staff as assistant first-team coach.

This meant I could continue in the game as I'd wanted, but that would be in the mornings – in the afternoons, I would fulfil a part-time role in the commercial department.

I already had a testimonial built into my contract because I took a pay cut when returning to the club from Manchester City. It had been agreed the deficit in wages would be made up in that game, with the club underwriting the difference plus an amount of money that I would be paid as compensation for loss of earnings.

Everything was agreed and I was as happy as I could be under the circumstances. I eventually had the major operation I'd needed on my knee, but the procedure only helped a bit and I've never been able to fully extend the joint since.

There are still bumps and crunches all over the place and the original diagnosis that I wouldn't be able to play again has proved spot-on.

Even though I was 99% sure my career was finished, it still came as a blow when that last flickering hope was extinguished.

But just as things had settled down and I knew where I

stood, out of the blue, Venables became the new owner when he bought Portsmouth for £1 in February 1997. Everything changed again at the club, with knock-on effects that would cause me no end of stress and hassle.

The thing about Terry is he is very hard to dislike. He's a charmer, talks easily to people – particularly the media – and it is a real skill of his. But for all his patter and likeability, I was never quite sure where he was coming from.

He arrived at Portsmouth spinning a number of plates. His acrimonious battle with Sir Alan Sugar at Spurs had cost him a small fortune as they fought one another in the courts.

He'd done fire-fighting jobs at Middlesbrough and Leeds United and now he'd bought Portsmouth for a quid. Because he had managed QPR under the chairmanship of Jim Gregory, he knew Martin Gregory well and they probably thought he was the ideal man to turn to.

Terry Fenwick, I'm certain, would have been happy that Venables was on board because his past relationship with him could only strengthen his position as manager.

However, for me his arrival meant a lot of extra headaches, even though whenever we spoke, we got on quite well.

By that point, the club had received the surgeon's report to say I was officially finished. In my contract, it stated that if you couldn't play anymore, they only had to pay you six months' money. So already the coaching/commercial department agreement I had in place was under threat because there had been an overlap between Venables buying the club and my new role being agreed.

Venables sniffed blood and armed with the surgeon's report saying I was finished, tried to use that against me, but it would mean they would have to renege on the gentleman's agreement we had. Eventually, I had to get the PFA to step in when Venables tried to invoke the six-month rule, despite the fact we'd already agreed otherwise.

It pissed me off no end but PFA boss Gordon Taylor came down to Scribes Club in London where we met Venables to try and thrash the matter out.

It was getting quite heated at one stage, so Taylor sent me to the bar to calm down a bit because I felt like swinging for Venables if truth be told.

What was grating me was that he didn't even try and understand my situation and the reasons I'd returned to Portsmouth in the first place. I'd taken £50,000 a year less to go back to Fratton Park with the proviso the testimonial would be worth £150,000, which the club would underwrite should there be a shortfall in revenue.

That was the deal and as far as I was concerned, that was set in stone – but Venables didn't even want to honour the testimonial game!

I was already in a relatively dark place dealing with the end of my playing career and now I felt he was taking the piss. I was not in the mood for any of these antics.

So with the testimonial in doubt, there was tension between me and Venables, who wanted to give me six months' notice on top of everything else. Not quite the charming man in reality but very money-driven individual.

Fortunately, the PFA wouldn't let that happen because everything had already been approved at board level. That came as a massive relief. It was a mess, but the fact was there was nothing Venables could do about it.

I accepted that there was no way I could do any sort of job under him, coaching or otherwise, and he reluctantly gave the testimonial the go-ahead.

He also agreed to give me the lump sum I was supposed to receive – but with the caveat that it would now be paid over 36 monthly instalments. I discovered the club had already cashed in the insurance policy the club had on me, which was a little premature by my thinking.

Typically, an insurance firm would come in with an initially lower offer of maybe 60% of the claim that was £600,000, which I'd say anyone with any brains would turn down.

But Venables must have bitten their hand off. After he accepted £360,000, the insurance no longer covered the pay-off I was due, which was £420,000 along with the testimonial and the job. He should have held out for a better offer from the insurers, but he took it and put it into the pot.

Venables left after 11 months as chairman at Fratton Park with a hefty bonus being paid to his company Vencorp during that time – at least that's what I read in the papers. I can't confirm the amount or that it actually happened, but as I say, it was widely reported at the time.

Also, you'd have to ask whether there was potential for a conflict of interests when he was at Pompey. He was also Australia's national coach and around that time we signed four or five Australian players on more than decent contracts.

They were all signed through Vencorp who reportedly took a healthy commission in August 1997 – a £300,000 'one-off performance bonus' – whatever that meant. In any other world, would that be allowed to happen? It seemed like a mess to me – with the club and yours truly caught the middle of everything.

Away from all the behind-the-scenes squabbling, Pompey did well during 1996/97, reaching the quarter-finals of the FA Cup and just finishing outside the play-offs.

But the following season was a disaster and by January 1998, Terry Fenwick had left. Venables followed him out of the door after being summoned to appear in the High Court by the Department of Trade and Industry, but not before he accepted a six-figure cash sum for his controlling interest in the club.

Alan Ball returned to Fratton Park as Fenners' replacement. He'd been sacked by City having taken the club down from the top flight and now Pompey were also seemingly heading for relegation from the second tier.

The club was already down to the bare bones financially and barely keeping its head above water. Then with just two of my compensation payments banked, the unthinkable happened and the club went into administration. As far as I knew, I was up the creek without a paddle and wondering whether things could possibly get any worse.

After my injury, nothing seemed was straightforward anymore at Pompey, not least my testimonial, which became a real ball-ache as well.

It was arranged for May 1998, a Bank Holiday Monday and, the way things were looking, it would be the day after the club either avoided relegation or survived. If things went to form, I already knew what the outcome would be.

The game itself was a right pain in the arse to arrange because it wasn't simply a manager bringing another team to play Pompey at Fratton Park. It was an 'Allstar XI' and that meant I had start ringing around individuals to see if they would play.

I was trying to get Chris Waddle, John Barnes, Gazza and

Mick Harford to come down because I knew they would add numbers on at the gate. Gazza agreed to play and because he did, singer Robbie Williams said he'd take part and so did TV presenter Chris Evans.

It wasn't easy and a bit of a nightmare to organise in all honesty, as was the sponsorship side of the game. But it had to be done, as I needed that final pay-off to help buffer me for whatever lay next in my life outside the game.

I had a committee to help with certain aspects, but there were some things that I needed to do on my own. Martin Gregory was still the chairman at this point, as he'd had to take temporary control again after Venables left until a new buyer was found. Though potential buyer Milan Mandaric was poised to take over, it was safe to assume he'd been waiting to see which division the club would be in before committing himself.

On the Friday before the testimonial was due to be played, Gregory got one of his 'associates' to hand me a message – presumably because he didn't have the balls to do it himself – telling me the game was off unless I agreed to sign a new deal regarding gate receipts and any potential short-falls.

The basic details said that if there was a deficit in revenue from the £150,000 we'd agreed when I returned to Portsmouth, the club now wouldn't have to make it up.

This was the day before the club's fate was decided. He was worried that if Portsmouth were relegated, there would be a downbeat feeling around the club and not many people would turn up to my game.

I had my hands tied at that late stage as I knew if it didn't happen on the following Monday, it would never happen. So I was forced to accept the terms but it was another devious, underhand tactic that had become typical of my second stay at the club. From a business point of view, I knew Gregory thought maybe just 5,000 would turn up if they'd been relegated and he'd be left with £100,000 to find for a club who were already on their knees. So even though I was livid, I knew why he'd done it.

As it turned out, a 3-1 win at Bradford City meant the club survived by the skin of their teeth. That result relegated my old club Manchester City in the process, along with Ball's other former team Stoke City. He'd had the last laugh on the two clubs that had sacked him.

On the Bank Holiday Monday, I was preparing for my testimonial and praying for good weather, which we were lucky to get. Everybody was in party mood because we'd stayed up and it was a massive relief to discover 13,000 Pompey fans had turned out.

I actually made more money than the underwritten amount and Alan Ball used the day as a sort of survival party celebration, so everyone was happy.

People tend to think that testimonials are an extra payment – a bonus of sorts – but in this instance, this was the money I hadn't had in wages in the first place. So it had been a lot of extra hassle to get what I should have been paid anyway, but by that point I just wanted to get the game done so I could finally move on.

It was a great day in many respects but I'd become worn down by all the politics and mind games that had been played before. That meant what should have been an enjoyable, stress-free goodbye to the supporters was anything but.

That said, I would officially like to thank everybody who

contributed to the day. The Pompey fans were fantastic, as they had been from day one, so it was at least a happy memory to take away with me.

As for my football career, that was pretty much it and I now had to face up to life outside the game. Fortunately, the footballer creditor rule that people often moan about when clubs go under was in place to protect me. When Milan Mandaric finally stepped in to bail the club out in summer 1998, he had to honour the pay-off I'd been originally promised before the club went belly up. The insurance pay-off I was entitled to was finally settled as well, but it all left a bitter taste.

The legal issues, administration, endless arguments and testimonial arrangements had taken up most of the previous two years but all that was now at an end. It was time to get busy either making a career somewhere else in the game or leaving football behind completely. I was at a crossroads in my life and I hadn't got a clue which path to take.

20

Building Blocks

There were a few offers on the table as I pondered my next move and some of the options sounded interesting, particularly an approach from Rushden and Diamonds, who wanted me to be their next manager. But the reality wasn't quite as straightforward as it seemed. I went along for a chat with Roger Ashby, the guy who was managing the club at the time, which I thought was a bit odd as he was still in situ.

My suspicions were proved correct as it turned out the whole thing was nothing more than a ruse. Ashby told me that he felt he'd taken the club as far as he could and it needed a different voice to take things forward.

He showed me around the ground and I have to admit I was impressed with the facilities and the all-round set-up of the club.

WALSHY

I told him I was interested. He said, 'There's just one proviso' at which point I was thinking, 'Here we go'... then he added, 'You've got to play.'

I asked Ashby if there was a difference, physically, between playing in the Conference and Division One and he said, 'Yes, it's harder,' and I thought, 'Well I'd still be playing now if I could manage playing at Conference level, wouldn't I, you idiot?'

I kept my thoughts to myself as I needed to keep my options open. I could have bullshitted my way through by saying I'd take it on and that I'd play the odd game, but I didn't really have the stomach to do that.

So although it could have been an interesting challenge, I was only interested in the managing side and that clearly wasn't exactly what they were offering.

I continued to explore new avenues. My accountant of 30 years, Bernie Hoffman, and another good friend, Richard Nugent, who was a financial advisor, wanted me to become a football agent.

We'd all worked in football for many years and had good contacts within the game so together, we decided to give it a go. The first player I had on my books was Lee Bradbury and my first deal was the one that took him from Portsmouth to Manchester City.

I didn't offer him to City, but on the back of half a good season at Pompey, City manager Frank Clark wanted to pay £3m for him – well above his market value.

Eric Hall came along to discuss the deal at Maine Road as I didn't have all the necessary licences at that point and I was staggered by what I saw. Bradbury had been on £25,000 a year at Portsmouth but City offered him £5,000 per week straight away – ten times what he'd been on at Fratton Park. I couldn't believe City didn't come in with an offer of around £150,000 per year, depending on him reaching certain targets.

We'd have still had to say yes to that offer because it was a great opportunity for Lee, but because City came in so high, we knew we could probably bump it up even more. After negotiations, he ended up with something like £6,500 per week – I thought the world really had gone mad.

I think City thought they had to pay a wage that somehow related to the hefty transfer fee, when in truth they didn't. As it was, Lee went to City and had a bad time of it, which proved it had been a hasty move by Clark. He should have waited to see whether he could follow up that impressive season the following year to lessen the risk.

Clark had believed Bradbury was the next Alan Shearer, but the truth was, he wasn't. Nowhere near, in fact.

The whole episode reminded me of Guy Whittingham, who had gone to Aston Villa on the back of a great season at Pompey but never seemed able to hold a place down as a front man. Things had gone sideways after that as he was played on the right side of midfield.

I did one or two other less high-profile deals but I was already thinking maybe that line of work wasn't for me. I think Richard Nugent felt I was putting more energy into trying to get into TV and media work than the agency role, but the truth is that I was working hard on both fronts. I was also developing what had been sort of a hobby by expanding the property business I had set up.

I guess I was trying to make sure the family could continue the lifestyle they were used to – or something as close to it as possible – but it wasn't easy. Your whole life changes and I didn't really enjoy the first few years out of the game at all. I covered a couple of games for Sky Sports and probably rushed into it. Looking back, I was depressed without realising it, because I still hadn't properly got my head around my career being over.

I just wanted to find something I was happy doing and was panicking a bit. I remember turning up for Sky at a game having done hardly any homework or research. I hadn't given the game any thought at all.

I didn't even want to be there, but I had to do something and I just about pulled it off. I did a couple of games and I don't think I was that good. When you don't have the facts and stats, you end up stuttering and winging your way through the live updates – and viewers aren't stupid.

I had my opinions but they were lacking detail and I should have waited until I felt ready to dive in. I did a bit of work for ITV Digital, Eurosport and some radio spots as I looked to gain more experience. Gradually, I started to get into it and felt I was improving.

Late in 1998, I began working occasionally at Meridian TV, which is based in Southampton. Gazza was playing for Middlesbrough at the time. He was in town having just played the Saints at The Dell, where the teams had drawn 3-3.

Gazza and Jimmy were going to stay the night at my house so I told them to pick me up at Meridian on their way past. When they got there, Jimmy was driving a battered old Ford. There were no airs or graces about Gazza, who looked just as comfortable as if he was in a stretch limo.

As we approached the village I live in, Gazza said that he needed to stop at the pub to get something. I told him he wasn't drinking at my house but he said he just wanted a crate of Red Bull. I went and got it for him and later we were just sat at the house watching TV, sipping Red Bull and by Gazza's standards, he was very quiet.

I knew he was on anti-depressants by that point so maybe they were having a calming effect on him, but whatever it was, he just wasn't himself. We went for a long walk along the river with Jimmy and chatted about old times but he was still subdued.

Later that night, a friend of the family was having a bonfire party and Gazza and Jimmy came along. Gazza was absolutely brilliant and back to the lad I'd known at Spurs.

He was sitting at the piano and he was a magnet for the kids, who he sang songs with. He just acted his usual daft-as-a-brush self. He had time for everyone – that was the side everyone loved and wanted to be around.

A picture was taken with everyone at the piano and my lads look back on that picture with a lot of affection. I suppose that's the last time I really saw him full of life and happy.

He was trying not to drink and it must have been hard for him. I just hoped he could keep on the right path, but as we all know, it didn't turn out that way.

A week later, Middlesbrough were playing Charlton and I went to see my mum and dad and then went over to the hotel Gazza was staying at. He was rooming with Andy Townsend so I had a chat with them, a cup of tea and then set off to watch the game at The Valley.

It was a surreal experience and I remember Gazza being substituted. I could see he was crying as he came off. He looked terrible. He couldn't run, he had been getting knocked over easily and looked an emotional wreck.

It was just sad to see him like that and it was even sadder to see the downward spiral he was on and has never really managed to get out of.

Part of me feels sorry for him, but part of me is angry because I look at the opportunities he had once he'd finished playing and just think, 'You know what mate? You could have had the best life ever.'

He had so much goodwill aimed in his direction that he could have turned up and just been Gazza and still got great money for being himself – people loved him.

He just needed his faculties and to stay sober then he'd have had a fantastic media career.

The truth is, it's hard for everyone when they come out of the game and there are plenty of players who have had the same problems but were given fewer opportunities. Don't get me wrong though, he deserved every opportunity coming his way because of the great player he was and the entertainment he'd given football fans up and down the country over the years.

We'd never really seen the likes of Paul Gascoigne before, but he paid a heavy price for his fame and talent, not unlike George Best and a host of other mavericks before him. From that point of view, part of me wants to slap him and tell him to get his life back on track, because I believe he could still have those opportunities. It's never too late.

My own media career was ticking along in the background as I continued to look at my own opportunities in the game. I was learning about the building industry, too, and the possibility of that being another source of income.

The house I'd had built was okay, but I discovered the builder had taken a lot of liberties. So when I moved into our new home

BUILDING BLOCKS

I decided to buy the house next door, knocked it down and built two new houses, selling one and living in the other while getting a guy called Kurt Brown to project-manage for me.

The housing market was on the up and I made some decent money – enough to continue and expand my interest in the trade without ever really diving headlong into it.

Things were gradually looking up and I could finally see a path forward away from the game, but with the good decisions came bad ones, too.

There was one business venture that went badly wrong involved a guy called Paul Garland, who was trying to get a veterans football business off the ground.

He'd got a few retired players on board and I agreed to give it a go and see how things went. We travelled as a team to a number of unusual venues around the world including an ice castle in Finland, gaining the confidence of the lads, before we travelled to Trinidad and Tobago for the main reason he'd got us all together – the Championship of Heroes.

We stayed in a nice hotel and played a bit of five-a-side. Garland was putting out the feelers for some big names to come on board as he looked to lift the profile.

Former Manchester United striker Dwight Yorke took part to add extra interest for the locals. Garland had got Jack Warner, former vice president of FIFA and president of CONCACAF on board and Paul Duffen, the future chairman of Hull City. Everything seemed pretty solid and above board.

Garland asked me to come on board as an investor and, after weighing up the potential, I put a substantial amount of my own money into the project, even though my accountant, who didn't like Garland and had a bad feeling about the investment, warned me not to. I didn't particularly like Garland either, but I did like the idea he was selling. The problem was I'd just made some money from the houses and I thought I had to start trusting my own gut instinct. I couldn't go running to my accountant every time I had an opportunity, because he would always err on the side of caution.

Different nations were coming on board and there was a lot of organisation needed but I was happy that Duffen was at the top of the pyramid, because I trusted his judgement and I thought he'd watch my back. For one reason or another, it didn't work out like that.

Garland lived in the affluent Cheshire suburb of Hale Barns at the time. The project hadn't been up and running for very long when I heard that he was now driving around the village in a new Bentley! All of a sudden my accountant's initial concerns seemed very well placed.

I flew out to Italy for the grand launch at the Savoy in Milan. At the top table were Ray Wilkins, Brazil legend Zico and Chuck Blazer, who recently turned informant against FIFA for the FBI. There were many other notable names along with the world's press, even though no player contracts had been secured as yet and the investors' money was steadily dwindling away.

I later met Jack Warner at a Park Lane hotel along with some others and everything seemed okay. Not long after, I learned that some of the money had supposedly been used to build a new stand at the venue the matches were due to be played at in Trinidad. However, I soon discovered (after a bit of digging) that the stand didn't actually exist at all!

This was despite the monies being transferred out to build it. I feared the worst but it was too late. I had a separate meeting with Jack Warner, who would later be accused of various fraudulent activities. He basically told us the whole project was about to collapse – which it did soon after.

I lost everything I'd put in but it wouldn't be the last time I had my fingers burnt.

I'd dived into a couple of other get-rich-quick deals. I dabbled in the stock market trying to make money off my own trades; attempted online share dealing and lost more money down the drain after another piece of poor judgement involving a guy called Peter Foster.

I'd met Foster in a bar with the Page 3 model Samantha Fox and he already had a reputation as being something of a ducker and diver. He'd been involved with various schemes such as herbal tea and dieting pills and was somebody my father-in-law had got to know.

Foster had gone to jail and my father-in- law had kept in touch with him to the point that when he was released, he went to stay with him for a short time while he got back on his feet.

While he'd been banged up, he'd dreamt up a new scheme so when he came out of jail all repentant and showing remorse for his previous crimes, everyone was sucked in by his promise to go straight and not get involved in any more dodgy deals.

It was all a front, however, as he laid the foundations for his next scam – one that would eventually put his name in the headlines alongside the then-prime minister Tony Blair! He began franchising all around the country and got in with Carole Caplin, health guru and advisor to Cherie Blair.

Foster then befriended her and the next thing he was up at Chequers staying with the Blairs, gaining credibility all the time. He sold £25,000 property franchises with all the money paid into an offshore tax haven off the coast of Australia. It wasn't long before people began to realise he couldn't keep his promises and became desperate to get their money back. People were queuing up to sell their story to the News of the World, Sunday People and the Mail – including me after I'd also been duped – to try to recoup their investment.

But the papers cleverly took a piece of each person's story to string into one feature that didn't cost them a penny.

It was a massively stressful period for me and, yet again, I'd had my fingers burnt. It taught me that there was no easy, fast way of making money and there was still no substitute for hard work.

Property was something I really enjoyed being involved in and so that's where I started to really concentrate my efforts. It's something I still enjoy doing today. Better still, it meant I was dealing in bricks and mortar, things that physically existed.

Of course, all the while I continued to work for Sky Sports. I have now been with them for eleven years and really enjoy being part of the team, commentating on games or occasionally reporting from the studio.

It's also good to be working with Phil Thompson again as he's a bloke I always liked from my days at Liverpool. I still can't help but give his nose stick though.

I remember he came into Sky one day looking all tanned and I asked him where he'd been. He said he'd been on a sunbed and I couldn't resist saying, 'How did you manage to get the lid down?' He gives as good as he gets, don't worry.

He always tells a story about a time he was at Anfield by the touchline and he starts hearing, 'Oi, sit down Pinocchio! Hey big nose, get back to the bench!'

BUILDING BLOCKS

He turned around to give him a mouthful back and realised it was a kid in a wheelchair who was absolutely caning him. What could he do? Like I said, Phil's a great lad.

There are a good bunch of guys at Sky Sports who do a great job and it's something I'm proud to be part of. Matt Le Tissier is a good lad, I've known Charlie Nicholas a long time because of the agent we briefly shared in the 1980s and I get on well with Alan McInally, Jeff Stelling and Paul Merson. Chris Kamara is as good as gold and a fantastic, funny lad.

The job has the occasional pitfalls, too. There was the occasion I said 'cunt' accidentally on live TV once. I remember saying it but I was trying to say 'can't', only for it to come out as 'cunt'. Some games you'll be at a game in the middle of winter and your feet are frozen and they will come to you for a link and you're so cold that your lips are quivering.

I've called Jeff Stelling 'Jess' on at least three occasions because the words sometimes just don't come out right. Still, it seems to have kept a few people happy on YouTube.

At home, my wife and two sons are settled, finding their own way in life near our home in Hampshire while my businesses are ticking along. Every now and then I see a YouTube clip of a goal I scored or a game I was involved in and I think, 'Christ, was that really me?'

I'm still involved with football, which I'm grateful for, but there's no substitute for playing. The nearest I get these days is with Liverpool Vets, which is something I really enjoy.

I get along really well with Ronnie Whelan, Alan Kennedy, David Johnson and Phil Neal, while it's also introduced me to some of the younger players I never had the chance to play with such as Robbie Fowler, Steve McManaman, Michael Thomas,

Rob Jones and Jason McAteer. I occasionally travel away with the Vets and there's always good banter, particularly between me and McAteer, who always suggests I'm wearing my son's clothes whenever we meet up. This invariably ends up with me hammering him for his fast receding hairline.

My knee does okay so long as the opposition aren't too hard – the moment it gets a bit physical, I start to struggle because I can't hold anybody off anymore.

I used to shield the ball by putting my arm out and planting my foot down so the whole distribution of power was focused in my knee, which just can't take that sort of strain anymore. It either gives way or I fall over. You just find a way of getting through the games and it's not really the football I go for. I just like being back with the lads, having a laugh and sharing a few beers over chats about our playing days.

We all get plenty of stick and it's great to still be able to do that from time to time.

I've thought about moving into coaching but in all honesty, I'm completely disillusioned with the coaching I've seen over the past few years. The mentality values that are promoted – the drive, desire, determination and competition – are just not what they used to be.

Heading is becoming a dying art and I don't see it being coached anywhere. The absolute basics that are the very building blocks of becoming a footballer – control, passing and heading – largely seem to be brushed over.

People should watch the header Lionel Messi scored in the 2009 Champions League final against Manchester United. He was almost 45 degrees ahead of the ball when he made contact but managed to hang in the air and nod into the far corner.

This is a guy not renowned for his heading ability but he still knows how to head a ball.

Certain clubs promote a certain way of playing throughout their age groups, but if a player leaves to go to a team that plays a different style, he may struggle because he's not been taught the very basics of the game. You can only be versatile if you have learned the basics and keep learning and improving them – the rest is up to how much the player really wants to succeed.

However, I think we all have ideas to right the wrongs in today's game, haven't we?

I'm glad I got the chance to do this book though, in truth, it's been an arduous project. I've tried to be as honest as I can throughout and, with me, what you see is what you get.

But don't believe everything you read in books – recently, there was a piece in Harry Redknapp's 2014 autobiography that pissed me off no end. He was talking about Gazza and asking where all his friends are now.

I have a suspicion Terry Venables is the source of a story he relates where he talks about a game for Spurs when we were away to Portsmouth in the FA Cup. One of the lads said to Terry he was worried about Gazza and that he didn't think he'd had any sleep.

Another of the lads told him Gazza had been up all night playing squash – I did mention earlier that he did everything back to front – so Venables asked who he'd been playing with. In Harry's book, I was supposedly the other player he'd been playing squash with – which is absolute bollocks!

Harry wrote that obviously one of the players had the metabolism to get up and play the next day; the other one was dropped from the squad because he would have been dead on his feet.

I found that particularly insulting because although I may not have been as good a player as Gazza was, I was certainly as fit as he was.

I sent out a tweet saying, 'Just been reading Harry's biography – correction: didn't even travel to Portsmouth – sounds like a load of Venners bullshit.'

I wasn't having a go at Harry because Venables is the only person he could have got that story from. I've got a feeling it might have been John Moncur who played squash that night but I'd have to ask him and find out for sure.

I wasn't even with the travelling party that day due to injury but I remember the game really well. Gazza scored twice during the game while Terry Fenwick broke his leg in the warm-up, which is quite an unusual thing to do. Anyway, that was then, this is now.

Looking back, I played for three of the biggest teams in the country and three clubs who weren't what you'd class as football powerhouses in English football, though I was equally proud to play for them.

Things could and maybe should have been different when I was at Liverpool and I allowed my time as Tottenham Hotspur to largely pass me by, but I would play some of the best football of my career towards the end of it at Manchester City and Portsmouth.

I made some good decisions along the way and some lousy ones, too, but don't we all do that in life at some point?

On the pitch, what I lacked in inches I tried to make up in tenacity, effort and skill. I still get a buzz when people tell me they used to enjoy watching me play for their club because it means a lot to me.

BUILDING BLOCKS

I suppose when I get Spurs fans telling me they have fond memories of me playing at White Hart Lane, I get a twinge of disappointment because I'm the first to admit that I could have done so much more had I been living my life the right way.

But it's still good that I managed to please some of the Spurs fans and it makes me wonder how good that period of my career could have been.

Challenged by my height and weight, if you'd said to me as a 14-year-old kid that I would have done what I did in the game as a player, I would have bitten your arm off and taken it without question. But when I remember the periods where I wasn't at my best, particularly at Tottenham, I know there were times during my 18 years in the game where I let myself down.

With the ability I had plus the drive and determination I possessed, I actually feel slightly disappointed that I didn't do better. I represented some of the biggest clubs in the land and also played for my country, but it should have been better.

Had I had the right breaks, I could have been at Liverpool a lot longer and maybe forced my way back into the England team, and I should have made a better fist of the hand I'd been dealt.

I made so many mistakes but I achieved most of the dreams I harboured as a kid and I hope I entertained a few people along the way. Ultimately, I think that's what really matters.

Index

249

INDEX

INDEX

INDEX

INDEX

INDEX